TRIPLE TESTED · FOR YOUR SUCCESS EVERY TIME

I hope that *Creative Cooking on a Budget* will excite and inspire each and every one of you to head for your kitchen and start cooking up a storm! Convenience foods and ready-to-eat meals abound these days but bear in mind that the cost of any time saved using them is greatly outweighed by their expense ... to say nothing of the fact that none is a match for the food you prepare yourself. From soup to dessert, everything tastes better if it's made by you.

Pamela Clark

FOOD EDITOR

CREATIVE COOKING ON A BUDGET

Creative Cooking on a Budget...

Coming up with ideas for economical meals that are both delicious and different from one another can be challenging fun and creatively satisfying ... there's nothing to beat the feeling of presenting a world-class dinner and knowing it didn't cost the earth. This gem of a cookbook contains a wealth of recipes that can be mixed and matched to make a treasure chest of meals, all destined to become firm family favourites that won't break the bank.

Chicken Osso Buco, page 55

Gingery Pineapple Cake with Cinnamon Custard, page 94

Seafood Laksa with Garlic Roti, page 10

Contents

Meatballs, Ratatouille and Ricotta Rice Cake, page 34

BRITISH & NORTH AMERICAN READERS:
Please note that Australian cup and spoon measurements are metric. A quick conversion guide appears on page 119. A glossary explaining unfamiliar terms and ingredients begins on page 113.

When soup and bread make the meal

Charmingly unaffected and comprised of ingredients we usually keep in the pantry or refrigerator, soothing soups and savoury breads form the backbone of a meal – and stroke the spirit of cook and diner alike

PASTA, PEA AND HAM SOUP WITH CARAWAY BEER BREAD

We used penne in this recipe but you can substitute it with any short pasta, even macaroni.

1 tablespoon vegetable oil
1 medium (150g) brown onion,
   chopped coarsely
2 large (360g) carrots,
   chopped coarsely
2 trimmed (150g) celery sticks,
   chopped coarsely
2 large (600g) potatoes,
   chopped coarsely
1.2kg ham bones
1¼ cups (250g) green split peas
2.5 litres (10 cups) water
2 cups (180g) penne

CARAWAY BEER BREAD

3¼ cups (485g) self-raising flour
2 teaspoons salt
2 teaspoons sugar
2 teaspoons caraway seeds
2 tablespoons finely chopped
   fresh chives
2 tablespoons finely chopped
   fresh parsley
375ml light beer

Heat oil in large pan; cook onion, carrot, celery and potato, stirring, until vegetables are browned lightly. Add bones, peas and the water to pan; bring to boil. Simmer, covered, about 1 hour or until peas are tender. Remove bones from soup, remove meat from bones; chop meat roughly, discard bones. Return meat to pan, stir until heated through. *[Can be made ahead to this stage. Cover; refrigerate overnight or freeze.]* Add pasta; simmer, uncovered, about 20 minutes or until pasta is tender. Serve soup with Caraway Beer Bread.

Caraway Beer Bread Grease two 14cm x 21cm loaf pans, line bases with baking paper. Combine flour, salt, sugar, seeds and herbs in large bowl. Make a well in centre of flour mixture; pour in beer all at once. Using a spoon, mix to a soft sticky dough. Knead dough on floured surface until smooth; divide in half. Knead each half lightly then place in prepared pans. Bake in moderate oven about 50 minutes or until bread is browned and sounds hollow when tapped. Turn onto wire rack to cool. *[Best made on day of serving.]*

FRENCH ONION SOUP WITH CHEESE CROUTONS

1kg meaty beef bones
2 medium (240g) carrots,
**   chopped coarsely**
2 trimmed (150g) celery sticks,
**   chopped coarsely**
1 medium (350g) leek,
**   chopped coarsely**
2 tablespoons tomato paste
1 medium (150g) brown
**   onion, quartered**
5 litres (20 cups) cold water
40g butter
5 large (1kg) brown onions,
**   chopped coarsely, extra**
1 clove garlic, crushed
1 tablespoon plain flour

CHEESE CROUTONS
1 small French bread stick
3/4 cup (90g) coarsely grated
**   cheddar cheese**

Place bones, carrot, celery, leek, paste and quartered onion in large oiled baking dish; bake, uncovered, in hot oven about 1 hour or until bones and vegetables are well browned.

Transfer bones and vegetables to large pan, add the water, bring to boil; simmer, uncovered, 3 hours. Strain into large heatproof bowl; cover, refrigerate stock overnight. *[Must be made ahead to this stage. Cover; refrigerate up to 2 days or freeze.]*

Heat butter in large pan; cook chopped onion and garlic, stirring, over low heat about 20 minutes or until onion is browned lightly. Add flour; cook, stirring, 1 minute. Remove and discard fat from surface of stock. Add stock gradually to pan, stirring; bring to boil. Simmer, uncovered, 5 minutes. *[Can be made ahead to this stage. Cover; refrigerate overnight.]* Serve onion soup topped with Cheese Croutons.

Cheese Croutons Cut bread into 2cm slices; sprinkle with cheese, grill until cheese melts.

SERVES 4

WINTER VEGETABLE SOUP WITH CHEESY CHIVE MUFFINS

2 tablespoons vegetable oil
4 cloves garlic, crushed
1 large (500g) leek,
**   chopped coarsely**
1 large (500g) kumara,
**   chopped coarsely**
2 medium (240g) carrots,
**   chopped coarsely**
4 large (720g) parsnips,
**   chopped coarsely**
2 (150g) celery sticks, chopped
300g pumpkin, chopped coarsely
1.75 litres (7 cups) chicken stock

CHEESY CHIVE MUFFINS
2 cups (300g) self-raising flour
100g butter, chopped coarsely
3/4 cup finely chopped fresh chives
2 tablespoons poppy seeds
1/2 teaspoon dried chilli flakes
1 cup (125g) finely grated
**   cheddar cheese**
2 eggs, beaten lightly
1 cup (250ml) buttermilk
2 tablespoons vegetable oil

Heat oil in large pan; cook garlic and leek, stirring, until leek is soft. Add remaining ingredients; simmer, uncovered, about 40 minutes or until vegetables are tender.

Blend or process mixture, in batches, until pureed. *[Can be made ahead to this stage. Cover; refrigerate overnight or freeze.]* Return soup to pan, stir over heat until hot; serve with Cheesy Chive Muffins.

Cheesy Chive Muffins Grease Texas-style 6-hole (3/4-cup/180ml-capacity) muffin pan. Place flour in large bowl; rub in butter, stir in chives, poppy seeds, chilli and cheese. Stir in combined remaining ingredients, taking care not to overmix. Divide mixture among pan holes; bake in moderately hot oven about 30 minutes or until browned. Turn muffins onto wire rack to cool.

SERVES 6

Left French onion soup with cheese croutons
Right Winter vegetable soup with cheesy chive muffins

HEARTY MINESTRONE WITH CHEESY GARLIC BREAD

- 1 tablespoon olive oil
- 1 medium (150g) white onion, sliced thickly
- 1 medium (120g) carrot, chopped coarsely
- 1 medium (350g) leek, sliced thickly
- 2 small (240g) potatoes, chopped coarsely
- 100g green beans, halved
- 2 trimmed (150g) celery sticks, chopped coarsely
- 2 cloves garlic, crushed
- 1.5 litres (6 cups) chicken stock
- 400g can tomatoes
- 2 tablespoons tomato paste
- 3/4 cup (135g) macaroni
- 2 small (180g) zucchini, chopped coarsely

CHEESY GARLIC BREAD

- 8 (150g) thick slices Italian-style bread
- 1/4 cup (60ml) olive oil
- 2 cloves garlic, crushed
- 1/2 cup (60g) finely grated cheddar cheese

Heat oil in large pan; cook onion, carrot, leek, potato, beans, celery and garlic, stirring, until onion is soft. Add stock, undrained crushed tomatoes and paste. Bring to boil; simmer, covered, stirring occasionally, about 45 minutes or until vegetables are tender. Add pasta and zucchini; boil, uncovered, for about 10 minutes or until pasta is tender. *[Can be made ahead to this stage. Cover; refrigerate overnight.]* Serve minestrone with Cheesy Garlic Bread.

Cheesy Garlic Bread Brush 1 side of bread slices with combined oil and garlic; grill or toast on both sides until browned lightly. Sprinkle with cheese, grill until cheese melts.

SERVES 4

ZUCCHINI SOUP WITH PARMESAN CROUTONS

- 1 tablespoon olive oil
- 1 medium (150g) brown onion, chopped finely
- 10 medium (1.2kg) zucchini, chopped coarsely
- 4 large (1.2kg) potatoes, chopped coarsely
- 1.5 litres (6 cups) chicken stock
- 1/2 cup (125ml) cream

PARMESAN CROUTONS

- 1 small French bread stick
- 2 tablespoons olive oil
- 1/2 cup (40g) finely grated parmesan cheese

Heat oil in large pan; cook onion, stirring, until soft. Add zucchini and potato; cook, stirring, 3 minutes. Stir in stock, bring to boil; simmer, uncovered, about 30 minutes or until potato is tender. Blend or process mixture, in batches, until smooth. *[Can be made ahead to this stage. Cover; refrigerate overnight.]*

Return soup to pan, stir in cream; cook, without boiling, until hot. Serve soup topped with Parmesan Croutons.

Parmesan Croutons Slice bread thinly; brush slices both sides with oil. Grill slices both sides; top with cheese, grill until cheese melts.

SERVES 4

Left Hearty minestrone with cheesy garlic bread
Right from top Zucchini soup with parmesan croutons; Fishysoisse with chive cottage loaf

FISHYSOISSE WITH CHIVE COTTAGE LOAF

50g butter
2 medium (700g) leeks,
**   chopped coarsely**
4 medium (800g) potatoes,
**   chopped coarsely**
1.5 litres (6 cups) chicken stock
1 cup (250ml) milk
250g white fish fillets

CHIVE COTTAGE LOAF
3 teaspoons (10g) dried yeast
1/2 cup (125ml) warm water
2 teaspoons sugar
2 1/2 cups (375g) plain flour
1 teaspoon salt
30g butter
1/2 cup (125ml) milk
2 tablespoons finely chopped
**   fresh chives**

Heat butter in large pan; cook leek, stirring, until soft. Add potato and stock; simmer, covered, about 20 minutes or until potato is tender. Blend or process potato mixture, in batches, until smooth; return to pan. *[Can be made ahead to this stage. Cover; refrigerate overnight or freeze.]*

Heat milk in small pan; cook fish, covered, over low heat, until cooked through. Drain over small bowl; reserve milk. Flake fish; discard any bones or skin. Add fish and milk to potato mixture; cook, stirring, until hot. Serve soup with Chive Cottage Loaf.

Chive Cottage Loaf Combine yeast with the water and sugar in small bowl; whisk until yeast dissolves. Cover; stand in warm place about 10 minutes or until mixture is frothy.

Place flour and salt in large bowl. Stir in melted butter, milk, chives and yeast mixture; mix to a soft dough. Turn dough onto floured surface; knead for about 10 minutes or until dough is smooth and elastic. Place dough in large greased bowl, cover; stand in warm place about 1 hour or until dough has doubled in size. Knead dough on floured surface until smooth. Shape dough into 20cm round, place on oiled oven tray, cover; stand in warm place about 15 minutes or until almost doubled in size. Using a sharp knife, make diagonal slashes on top of bread; bake in moderately hot oven about 30 minutes or until loaf sounds hollow when tapped.

SERVES 4

SEAFOOD LAKSA WITH GARLIC ROTI

500g small black mussels
250g white fish fillets
1 tablespoon vegetable oil
1 medium (150g) onion,
  sliced thinly
2 tablespoons green curry paste
2 teaspoons ground turmeric
1 cup (130g) coconut milk powder
1 3/4 cups (430ml) water
1.5 litres (6 cups) chicken stock
85g instant noodles
1 tablespoon lemon juice
2 green onions, sliced thinly
2 tablespoons chopped fresh
  coriander leaves

GARLIC ROTI
3 cups (450g) plain flour
1 teaspoon sugar
1 teaspoon salt
1 egg, beaten lightly
1 clove garlic, crushed
3/4 cup (180ml) warm water,
  approximately
1/4 cup (60ml) vegetable oil

Scrub mussels; remove beards. Discard skin and bones from fish; chop fish coarsely.

Heat oil in large pan; cook onion, paste and turmeric, stirring, until onion is soft. Blend milk powder with the water; add mixture, along with stock, to pan, bring to the boil. Add mussels, fish and noodles to pan; simmer, uncovered, for about 5 minutes or until mussels open (discard any that do not). Stir in juice and green onion. Serve laksa, sprinkled with coriander, with Garlic Roti.

Garlic Roti Place flour, sugar and salt in large bowl; stir in egg, garlic and enough water to mix to a soft dough. Knead dough on floured surface about 10 minutes or until smooth and elastic, wrap in plastic; refrigerate 30 minutes. Divide dough into 12 portions; roll each portion on floured surface into 17cm round. Brush each round with a little of the oil; roll tightly, like a Swiss roll, then roll up both ends to meet in the centre. Wrap in plastic to prevent unrolling and drying out; repeat process with remaining rounds. Roll out each rolled portion again on floured surface into 17cm round; cook over high heat in large oiled heavy-base pan until puffed and browned both sides.

SERVES 4

TUSCAN BEAN SOUP WITH POTATO FOCACCIA

1½ cups (300g) dried
  haricot beans
1 tablespoon olive oil
1 medium (150g) brown onion,
  chopped coarsely
2 cloves garlic, crushed
2 trimmed (150g) celery sticks,
  chopped coarsely
1 medium (120g) carrot,
  chopped coarsely
2 bacon rashers, chopped coarsely
4 large (1kg) ripe tomatoes, peeled,
  chopped coarsely
1.5 litres (6 cups) vegetable stock
1 teaspoon sugar
¼ cup fresh parsley sprigs
¼ cup (60ml) tomato paste

POTATO FOCACCIA
2 cups (300g) plain flour
½ teaspoon salt
2 teaspoons (7g) dried yeast
2 tablespoons olive oil
1 cup (250ml) warm water
1 large (300g) potato, sliced thinly
1 tablespoon fresh rosemary
1 clove garlic, sliced thinly

Cover beans with water in large pan; stand, covered, overnight.

Heat oil in large pan; cook onion, garlic, celery, carrot and bacon, stirring, until vegetables are just tender. Add tomato; cook, stirring, about 5 minutes or until tomato is soft. Stir in rinsed drained beans, stock, sugar, parsley and paste, bring to boil; simmer, covered, about 1¼ hours or until beans are tender. *[Can be made ahead to this stage. Cover; refrigerate overnight or freeze.]* Serve soup with Potato Focaccia.

Potato Focaccia Place flour, salt and yeast in large bowl. Gradually stir in oil and water, mix to a soft dough. Knead dough on floured surface about 5 minutes or until smooth and elastic. Place dough onto oiled oven tray; press into 24cm round. Cover loosely with plastic wrap; stand in warm place about 1 hour or until doubled in size.

Remove plastic wrap from dough; top with potato then sprinkle with rosemary and garlic. Bake in hot oven about 25 minutes or until focaccia is just browned and sounds hollow when tapped. *[Can be made ahead to this stage. Cover; refrigerate overnight.]* Just before serving, place focaccia under hot grill about 3 minutes or until top is crisp.

SERVES 4

Left Seafood laksa with garlic roti
Right Tuscan bean soup with potato focaccia

ROAST PEPPER AND TOMATO SOUP WITH PESTO CROSTINI

We used the traditional pesto made with basil but you can try any variety you prefer.

4 medium (800g) red capsicums
1 tablespoon olive oil
1 large (200g) brown onion, chopped coarsely
2 cloves garlic, crushed
400g can tomatoes
1 litre (4 cups) chicken stock
8 black olives, seeded, sliced thinly

PESTO CROSTINI
1 small French bread stick
2 tablespoons olive oil
1/4 cup (60g) bottled pesto

Quarter capsicums, remove and discard seeds and membranes. Roast under grill or in very hot oven, skin-side up, until skin blisters and blackens. Cover capsicum pieces in plastic or paper for 5 minutes; peel away skin.

CLAM CHOWDER WITH GREEN ONION PANCAKES

Pipis or vongole can be substituted for the baby clams.

1kg baby clams
20g butter
1 large (200g) brown onion, chopped coarsely
2 large (600g) potatoes, chopped coarsely
2 tablespoons plain flour
2 cups (500ml) vegetable stock
2 cups (500ml) milk
2 bacon rashers, chopped coarsely
1/4 cup (60ml) lemon juice
1/2 cup (80g) fresh, canned or frozen corn kernels

GREEN ONION PANCAKES
1 cup (150g) plain flour
1 teaspoon salt
2 eggs, beaten lightly
1 cup (250ml) milk
2 green onions, chopped

Rinse clams under cold water; place in large bowl, sprinkle with salt, cover with cold water. Soak 1 1/2 hours; rinse, drain.

Heat butter in large pan; cook onion, stirring, until soft. Add potatoes and flour; cook, stirring, 1 minute. Stir in stock and milk; simmer, covered, about 20 minutes or until potato is soft. Blend or process 3/4 of the potato mixture, in batches, until smooth; return to pan with remaining potato mixture. *[Can be prepared ahead to this stage. Cover, separately; refrigerate overnight.]*

Cook bacon in small heated pan, stirring, until browned and crisp; drain on absorbent paper. Stir bacon, clams, juice and corn into potato mixture; simmer, covered, about 3 minutes or until clams open (discard any that do not). Serve chowder with Green Onion Pancakes.

Green Onion Pancakes Place flour and salt in medium bowl; gradually whisk in combined eggs and milk until mixture is smooth, stir in onion. Pour 1/4 cup of batter in medium heated oiled heavy-base pan; cook until browned lightly both sides. Repeat with remaining batter.

SERVES 4

Heat oil in large pan; cook onion and garlic, stirring, until onion is soft. Add capsicum, undrained crushed tomatoes and stock; simmer, covered, 20 minutes. Blend or process mixture, in batches, until pureed. [Can be made ahead to this stage. Cover; refrigerate overnight or freeze.] Return soup to pan; stir over heat until hot. Serve soup, sprinkled with olives, with Pesto Crostini.

Pesto Crostini Cut bread into 1cm slices; brush with oil both sides, grill until browned lightly. Spread with pesto.

SERVES 4

Left Clam chowder with green onion pancakes
Below Roast pepper and tomato soup with pesto crostini
Right Cauli-corn chowder with bacon and chive pancakes

CAULI-CORN CHOWDER WITH BACON AND CHIVE PANCAKES

20g butter
2 medium (300g) brown onions, chopped coarsely
2 tablespoons plain flour
1 small (1kg) cauliflower, chopped coarsely
1.5 litres (6 cups) chicken stock
420g can creamed corn

BACON AND CHIVE PANCAKES
2 bacon rashers, chopped finely
3/4 cup (110g) self-raising flour
2 eggs, beaten lightly
1/2 cup (125ml) milk
2 tablespoons finely chopped fresh chives

Heat butter in large pan; cook onion, stirring, until soft. Add flour; cook, stirring, 1 minute. Add cauliflower and stock, bring to boil; simmer, covered, about 30 minutes or until cauliflower is soft. Blend or process mixture, in batches, until pureed. [Can be made ahead to this stage. Cover; refrigerate overnight or freeze.] Return chowder to pan, stir in corn; stir over heat until hot. Serve chowder with Bacon and Chive Pancakes.

Bacon and Chive Pancakes Cook bacon, stirring, in medium heated pan until browned and crisp; drain on absorbent paper. Place flour in medium bowl, gradually whisk in combined eggs and milk until mixture is smooth; stir in bacon and chives. Reheat same pan; pour in 1/4 cup batter for each pancake, cook until browned lightly both sides. Repeat with remaining batter.

SERVES 4

CHICKEN VEGETABLE SOUP WITH FILLED PARATHA

1.6kg chicken
3 medium (450g) brown onions, chopped coarsely
3 trimmed (225g) celery sticks, chopped coarsely
1 teaspoon black peppercorns
1 bay leaf
4 litres (16 cups) water
2 teaspoons vegetable oil
1 medium (120g) carrot, chopped coarsely
1 clove garlic, crushed
2 small (180g) zucchini, chopped coarsely
250g spinach, chopped coarsely
1/2 cup (100g) couscous

FILLED PARATHA

3/4 cup (120g) wholemeal plain flour
3/4 cup (110g) plain flour
1 teaspoon salt
1 tablespoon butter
1/2 cup (125ml) water, approximately

1 medium (400g) kumara, chopped coarsely
1 medium (150g) brown onion, chopped finely
2 teaspoons ground cumin
2 teaspoons ground coriander
2 teaspoons hot paprika
1 tablespoon vegetable oil

Discard chicken skin; cut chicken into large pieces. Place chicken in large pan with 2/3 of the onion and celery, peppercorns, bay leaf and water; bring to boil. Simmer, uncovered, 2 hours.

Strain chicken mixture over large bowl; reserve liquid. Remove chicken flesh from bones; discard bones and vegetables. *[Best made ahead to this stage. Cover, separately; refrigerate overnight.]*

Skim off and discard fat from surface of stock. Heat oil in large pan; cook remaining onion and celery, carrot and garlic, stirring, until vegetables are just tender. Stir in zucchini, reserved stock and chicken flesh; bring to boil. Stir in spinach and couscous; simmer, 2 minutes or until couscous has softened. Serve soup with Filled Paratha.

Filled Paratha Process flours, salt and butter with enough water to form ball of dough. Knead dough on floured surface about 10 minutes or until smooth, wrap in plastic wrap; stand 1 hour.

Meanwhile, boil, steam or microwave kumara until tender; drain, mash in medium bowl. Cook onion and spices, stirring, in small heated oiled pan until onion is soft; stir mixture into kumara.

Divide dough into 8 portions; roll each portion on floured surface into 17cm round. Stack rounds between layers of plastic wrap to prevent drying out. Divide kumara mixture among 4 rounds; spread gently over rounds leaving a 1cm border. Brush around edges with water; top with remaining rounds, press edges together to seal. Heat oil in large pan; cook paratha, one at a time, until browned both sides. Drain on absorbent paper.

SERVES 4

Above Chicken vegetable soup with filled paratha
Right Kumara and meatball soup with cheese damper

KUMARA AND MEATBALL SOUP WITH CHEESE DAMPER

300g minced lamb
2 teaspoons finely grated
lemon rind
3 bird's-eye chillies, seeded,
chopped finely
1/2 cup finely chopped fresh chives
1 tablespoon olive oil
2 cloves garlic, crushed
4 small (400g) red onions,
chopped finely
1 teaspoon ground turmeric
2 teaspoons ground cumin
2 large (1kg) kumara,
chopped coarsely
3 cups (750ml) beef stock
1 litre (4 cups) water

CHEESE DAMPER

3 1/2 cups (525g) self-raising flour
1 teaspoon salt
1 1/2 tablespoons cracked
black pepper
1 tablespoon sugar
40g butter, softened
1/2 cup chopped fresh parsley
1 cup (125g) finely grated
cheddar cheese
1/2 cup (125ml) milk
1 cup (250ml) water, approximately

Combine lamb, rind, chilli and 2 tablespoons of the chives in medium bowl; mix well. Using hand, roll rounded teaspoons of mixture into balls. Place on tray, cover; refrigerate 1 hour. [Can be made ahead to this stage. Cover; refrigerate overnight or freeze.]

Heat oil in large pan; cook garlic, onion, turmeric and cumin, stirring, until onion is soft. Add kumara, stock, water and remaining chives, bring to boil; simmer, uncovered, about 40 minutes or until kumara is just tender. Add meatballs; boil about 5 minutes or until meatballs are cooked through. Serve soup with Cheese Damper.

Cheese Damper Place flour, salt, pepper and sugar in large bowl; rub in butter. Stir in parsley, cheese, milk and enough water to make a sticky dough. Turn dough onto floured surface; knead until just smooth. Place dough on oiled oven tray; press into 15cm round. Cut a cross on top of dough about 1cm deep. Brush dough with a little extra milk, sprinkle with a little extra flour. Bake in moderately hot oven about 40 minutes or until damper sounds hollow when tapped. Turn onto wire rack to cool.

SERVES 4 TO 6

CRISP SAUSAGE AND LENTIL SOUP

We used thin beef sausages, often labelled breakfast sausages, in this recipe but try any of the various types available.

1 tablespoon vegetable oil
3 cloves garlic, crushed
2 large (400g) brown onions, chopped coarsely
1.75 litres (7 cups) chicken stock
1¹/₂ cups (300g) brown lentils
3 large (750g) tomatoes, chopped coarsely
4 small (280g) carrots, chopped finely
5 trimmed (375g) celery sticks, chopped finely
8 (500g) thin beef sausages

Heat oil in large pan; cook garlic and onion, stirring, until onion is soft. Stir in stock, lentils, tomato, carrot and celery; simmer, uncovered, about 30 minutes or until lentils are just tender. *[Can be made ahead to this stage. Cover; refrigerate overnight or freeze.]*

Meanwhile, cook sausages, uncovered, in medium pan until browned all over and cooked through. Drain sausages on absorbent paper, slice then add to soup; cook, uncovered, until hot.

SERVES 4

CHICKPEA SOUP WITH CHEESE AND CAPSICUM PIDE

1¹/₂ cups (300g) dried chickpeas
1 tablespoon olive oil
2 large (400g) brown onions, chopped coarsely
2 cloves garlic, crushed
2 teaspoons ground cumin
1 medium (200g) red capsicum, chopped coarsely
415g can tomatoes
1.5 litres (6 cups) vegetable stock
1 medium (200g) potato, chopped coarsely
2 tablespoons lemon juice

CHEESE AND CAPSICUM PIDE
1 tablespoon olive oil
3 cloves garlic, crushed
2 medium (400g) red capsicums, sliced thickly
1 long loaf pide
2 cups (250g) coarsely grated cheddar cheese

Cover chickpeas with water in large bowl; stand, covered, overnight. Drain chickpeas; rinse under cold water, drain.

Heat oil in large pan; cook onion, garlic, cumin and capsicum, stirring, until onion is soft. Add chickpeas, undrained

crushed tomatoes and stock. Bring to boil; simmer, covered, about 1 hour or until chickpeas are tender. *[Can be made ahead to this stage. Cover; refrigerate overnight or freeze.]* Stir in potato; cook about 10 minutes or until tender. Just before serving, stir in juice. Serve soup, topped with reserved capsicum mixture (below), with Cheese and Capsicum Pide.

Cheese and Capsicum Pide Heat oil in large pan; cook garlic and capsicum, stirring over low heat, about 15 minutes or until capsicum is very soft. *[Can be made ahead to this stage. Cover; refrigerate overnight.]* Place bread on oven tray; sprinkle with cheese and 3/4 of capsicum mixture. Reserve remaining capsicum mixture to serve with soup. Bake in moderate oven about 10 minutes or until cheese melts.

SERVES 4

MULLIGATAWNY SOUP WITH PAPPADUMS

1 tablespoon vegetable oil
1 medium (150g) brown onion, chopped coarsely
2 cloves garlic, crushed
1/4 cup (60g) mild curry paste
1 large (200g) apple
1 medium (120g) carrot, chopped coarsely
1 medium (200g) potato, chopped coarsely
1/2 cup (100g) red lentils
1 litre (4 cups) chicken stock
1 tablespoon lemon juice
1/2 cup (65g) coconut milk powder
1 cup (250ml) water
1/4 cup (60ml) yogurt
8 pappadums
vegetable oil, for deep-frying

Heat oil in large pan; cook onion and garlic, stirring, until onion is soft. Add paste; cook, stirring, until fragrant. Coarsely grate enough peeled cored apple to make 2 tablespoons; reserve. Coarsely chop remaining apple; add to pan with carrot, potato, lentils and stock. Bring to boil; simmer, covered, about 15 minutes or until lentils and vegetables are tender.

Blend or process mixture, in batches, until pureed. *[Can be made ahead to this stage. Cover; refrigerate overnight or freeze.]* Return soup to pan, add juice and blended coconut milk powder and water; stir until hot. Serve soup, sprinkled with reserved apple and drizzled with yogurt, with pappadums.

Meanwhile, deep-fry pappadums in hot oil until puffed and crisp; drain on absorbent paper.

SERVES 4

Left from top Chickpea soup with cheese and capsicum pide; Crisp sausage and lentil soup
Above Mulligatawny soup with pappadums

BEEF AND BARLEY SOUP

1 tablespoon vegetable oil
2 medium (300g) brown onions,
   chopped finely
1 tablespoon dried tarragon
500g gravy beef, chopped coarsely
1/2 cup (100g) barley
3 cups (750ml) beef stock
3 cups (750ml) water
2 cups (500ml) water, extra
2 medium (400g) potatoes,
   chopped coarsely
2 medium (240g) carrots,
   chopped finely
2 medium (240g) zucchini,
   chopped finely
2 large (360g) parsnips,
   chopped finely
2 trimmed (150g) celery sticks,
   sliced thinly
2 tablespoons chopped
   fresh parsley
1 teaspoon salt
1 teaspoon cracked black pepper

Heat oil in large pan; cook onion and tarragon, stirring, until onion is soft. Add beef; cook, stirring, until browned all over. Add barley, stock and the water, bring to boil; simmer, covered, about 30 minutes or until barley is tender. *[Can be made ahead to this stage. Cover; refrigerate overnight or freeze.]* Stir in the extra water, potato, carrot, zucchini, parsnip and celery; simmer, covered, about 20 minutes or until beef is cooked through and tender. Just before serving, stir in parsley, salt and pepper. Serve with toast, if desired.

SERVES 4

PUMPKIN DHAL SOUP WITH PUMPKIN CORIANDER SCONES

1 cup (200g) toor dhal
   (yellow split peas)
1 tablespoon vegetable oil
2 medium (300g) brown onions,
   chopped finely
1 tablespoon ground turmeric
1 tablespoon ground cumin
1 tablespoon ground coriander
1 tablespoon yellow mustard seeds
1 tablespoon grated fresh ginger
1 litre (4 cups) chicken stock
1.3kg pumpkin
1 litre (4 cups) water
1 tablespoon vegetable oil, extra
1 teaspoon ground nutmeg

PUMPKIN CORIANDER SCONES
2 cups (300g) self-raising flour
1/4 cup finely chopped fresh
   coriander leaves
3/4 cup (180ml) buttermilk,
   approximately

Cover dhal with water; stand, covered, 2 hours or overnight.

Drain dhal; rinse under cold water, drain. Heat oil in large pan; cook onion, stirring, until soft. Add turmeric, cumin, coriander, seeds and ginger; cook, stirring, until fragrant. Stir in stock and dhal, bring to boil; simmer, uncovered, for 10 minutes.

Meanwhile, finely grate enough of the pumpkin to make 3 cups; coarsely chop remaining pumpkin. Add the water and half of the grated pumpkin to mixture in pan (reserve remaining grated pumpkin for scones, below); simmer, uncovered, about 30 minutes or until soup thickens. *[Can be made ahead to this stage. Cover; refrigerate overnight or freeze.]*

Combine chopped pumpkin and extra oil in baking dish, sprinkle with nutmeg; bake, uncovered, in moderately hot oven about 20 minutes or until browned and tender. Serve soup, topped with roasted pumpkin, with Pumpkin Coriander Scones.

Pumpkin Coriander Scones Grease 20cm round sandwich pan. Place flour in large bowl; stir in coriander and reserved half of the grated pumpkin, then enough buttermilk to mix to soft, sticky dough. Knead dough on floured surface about 5 minutes or until smooth and elastic. Press dough to 3cm thickness; cut into 5cm rounds. Place scones in prepared pan; bake in hot oven about 25 minutes or until scones sound hollow when tapped. Turn onto wire rack to cool.

SERVES 4 TO 6

SESAME PASTA BROTH

2 teaspoons peanut oil
2 medium (300g) brown onions,
  chopped coarsely
2 cloves garlic, crushed
1 medium (350g) leek, sliced
2 medium (220g) carrots, chopped
1 large (180g) parsnip, chopped
1 teaspoon black peppercorns
2 bay leaves
2.5 litres (10 cups) water
100g lasagne sheets
1 tablespoon soy sauce
1 tablespoon oyster sauce
4 bird's-eye chillies, seeded,
  chopped finely
4 canned anchovy fillets, drained,
  chopped finely
2 teaspoons sesame oil
300g choy sum, trimmed, chopped
200g bok choy, trimmed,
  chopped coarsely
2 green onions, sliced thinly

Heat peanut oil in large pan; cook brown onion, garlic and leek, stirring, until vegetables are soft. Add carrot, parsnip, peppercorns and bay leaves; cook, stirring, until vegetables are browned lightly. Add water, bring to boil; simmer, uncovered, 1½ hours, skimming broth occasionally. Drain over large pan; reserve broth. *[Can be made ahead to this stage. Cover; refrigerate overnight or freeze.]*

Break lasagne into large pieces. Bring broth to boil; add lasagne, sauces, chilli, anchovy and sesame oil. Boil, uncovered, about 10 minutes or until the lasagne is just tender. Add choy sum and bok choy; simmer, uncovered, until vegetables are just tender. Just before serving, stir in green onion.

SERVES 4

Far left Pumpkin dhal soup with pumpkin coriander scones
Left Beef and barley soup
Above Sesame pasta broth

SWEETCORN AND CHICKEN SOUP WITH POTATO CAKES

1 tablespoon vegetable oil
1 small (200g) leek, sliced thinly
4 (440g) chicken thigh fillets, sliced thinly
2 large (500g) corn cobs
1 litre (4 cups) chicken stock
2 x 130g cans creamed corn
3 green onions, sliced thinly

POTATO CAKES

3 large (900g) potatoes
1/4 cup (60ml) vegetable oil

Heat oil in large pan; cook leek, stirring, until soft. Add chicken; cook, stirring, until browned all over. Cut kernels from corn cobs; add to pan. Stir in stock and creamed corn, bring to boil; simmer, uncovered, about 20 minutes or until chicken is tender. Stir in onion; serve soup with Potato Cakes.

Potato Cakes Peel and coarsely grate potatoes; squeeze out excess moisture. Heat oil in medium heavy-base pan; add a quarter of the potato to pan, flatten slightly. Cook both sides until browned and cooked through; drain on absorbent paper. Repeat with remaining potato.

SERVES 4

HARIRA WITH SPICED PITTA

Harira is the Moroccan soup traditionally served at the end of the day during the month-long fasting period of Ramadan.

2 tablespoons olive oil
250g diced lamb
2 teaspoons ground coriander
2 teaspoons ground cumin
1/4 teaspoon ground clove
1 large (200g) brown onion, chopped coarsely
2 cloves garlic, crushed
400g can tomatoes
1 cup (200g) brown lentils
2 litres (8 cups) chicken stock
1/4 cup chopped fresh coriander leaves
1/4 cup chopped fresh parsley
1 tablespoon lemon juice

SPICED PITTA

2 teaspoons (7g) dry yeast
1 teaspoon sugar
11/4 cups (310ml) warm milk
41/4 cups (635g) plain flour
1 teaspoon salt
1/2 cup (125ml) yogurt
1 egg, beaten lightly
1/4 cup (60ml) water
1 tablespoon vegetable oil
1 teaspoon ground coriander
1 teaspoon ground cumin
1/2 teaspoon cracked black pepper

Combine half the oil, lamb, coriander, cumin and clove in large bowl; cover, refrigerate 6 hours or overnight. Heat remaining oil in large pan; cook onion and garlic, stirring, until onion is soft. Add lamb mixture; cook, stirring, until lamb is browned lightly. Add undrained crushed tomatoes, lentils, stock and herbs; simmer, covered, about 30 minutes or until lentils are tender. *[Can be made ahead to this stage. Cover; refrigerate overnight or freeze.]* Just before serving, stir in juice. Serve soup with Spiced Pitta.

Spiced Pitta Combine yeast, sugar and milk in small bowl; whisk until yeast dissolves. Cover; stand in warm place about 10 minutes or until mixture is frothy.

Place flour and salt in large bowl; stir in yeast mixture, yogurt, egg, water and oil, mix to a soft dough. Turn dough onto floured surface; knead about 10 minutes or until smooth and elastic. Place dough in large greased bowl, cover; stand in warm place about 1 hour or until doubled in size.

Turn dough onto floured surface, knead until smooth; divide dough into 8 portions. Knead each portion into a ball, place on floured tray, cover loosely with plastic wrap; stand in warm place about 30 minutes or until doubled in size.

Preheat oven to very hot. Roll each ball into a 25cm round; heat oven tray in very hot oven. Place 1 round at a time on tray; bake, on top shelf, about 5 minutes. Brush with combined oil, coriander, cumin and pepper; bake, uncovered, about 1 minute or until pitta is increased in size and browned lightly. Wrap pitta in a tea-towel to keep warm before serving.

SERVES 4

Opposite Sweetcorn and chicken soup with potato cakes
Below Harira with spiced pitta

Delicious dishes from a variety of cuts

Many of the tastiest meat dishes have peasant origins, so choosing an economical form of beef, pork or lamb – from mince to offal to the scrumptious bony bits – is in keeping with the best culinary traditions

STEAK, KIDNEY AND MUSHROOM PIE

3 cups (450g) plain flour
2 egg yolks
125g lard
2/3 cup (160ml) water
1 egg, beaten lightly

BEEF FILLING
300g beef kidneys
1kg beef chuck steak, cubed
1/4 cup (60ml) vegetable oil
3 cloves garlic, crushed
2 large (400g) brown onions, chopped
200g button mushrooms, halved
2 teaspoons dried tarragon leaves
2 cups (500ml) beef stock
1 tablespoon Worcestershire sauce
1/4 cup (35g) plain flour
1/2 cup (125ml) water

Grease 1.25-litre (5-cup capacity) ovenproof dish.

Place flour in large bowl; add egg yolks, cover with some of the flour. Heat lard with the water in small pan until melted; bring mixture to boil then pour all at once into flour mixture, stirring to a firm dough. Knead dough on bench until smooth, cover; refrigerate 15 minutes.

Roll 2/3 of pastry on bench until large enough to line prepared dish. Lift pastry into dish, ease into side; trim edge. Cover; refrigerate 30 minutes.

Spoon Beef Filling into pastry case, brush edge of pastry with egg. Roll remaining pastry on bench until large enough to cover filling. Lift pastry over filling, trim edge, press edge to seal; brush top with egg. Bake in hot oven about 45 minutes or until browned.

Beef Filling Cut kidneys in half, remove fat and membranes; rinse kidney under cold water, drain, chop coarsely.

Heat 2 tablespoons of the oil in large pan; cook beef, in batches, until browned all over. Add remaining oil to same pan; cook garlic, onion, mushrooms and tarragon, stirring, until onion is soft. Return beef to pan with kidney, stock and sauce. Bring to boil; simmer, covered, about 1 hour or until beef is tender. Stir in blended flour and water; stir over heat until mixture boils and thickens, cool. *[Can be made ahead to this stage. Cover; refrigerate up to 2 days or freeze.]*

SERVES 4

OXTAIL WITH CRISPY BACON

2kg oxtail
1/3 cup (50g) plain flour
2 tablespoons olive oil
1 1/2 cups (375ml) dry red wine
4 medium (760g) tomatoes,
chopped coarsely
2 cloves garlic, crushed
200g black olives, seeded,
chopped coarsely
2 tablespoons finely chopped
fresh oregano
1/3 cup finely chopped fresh parsley
8 bacon rashers

Toss oxtail in flour; shake off excess. Heat oil in large flameproof baking dish; cook oxtail, in batches, until browned all over. Add wine, tomatoes and garlic; simmer, stirring, 2 minutes. Return oxtail to dish with olives, oregano and parsley. Bake, covered, stirring occasionally, in slow oven about 3 hours or until oxtail is tender. *[Can be made a day ahead. Cover; refrigerate or freeze.]* Just before serving, halve bacon lengthways; grill until browned and crisp, serve with oxtail.

SERVES 4

BEEF AND BLACK-BEAN STIR-FRY

500g beef round steak, sliced thinly
2 cloves garlic, crushed
2 teaspoons grated fresh ginger
2 tablespoons lime juice
1/2 teaspoon sugar
1 tablespoon peanut oil
1 large (200g) brown onion,
sliced thickly
400g broccoli florets
2 large (360g) carrots, sliced thinly
1/3 cup (80ml) black-bean sauce
1 tablespoon soy sauce
1 teaspoon cornflour
2 tablespoons water
2 teaspoons finely grated lime rind

Combine beef, garlic, ginger, juice and sugar in medium bowl; mix well. Cover; refrigerate 4 hours or overnight. *[Can be made ahead to this stage. Cover; freeze if desired.]* Heat half the oil in wok or large pan; stir-fry beef mixture, in batches, until browned.

Heat remaining oil in same pan; stir-fry onion, broccoli and carrot about 2 minutes or until vegetables are just soft. Return beef to pan; stir-fry with blended sauces, cornflour and the water about 2 minutes or until mixture comes to boil and thickens slightly. Serve sprinkled with rind.

SERVES 4

BUBBLE AND SQUEAK PIE

This is a delicious way of making a meal out of leftover vegetables from last night's dinner. For this recipe, you will need five cooked tiny new potatoes, one 200g piece cooked pumpkin and one medium cooked carrot.

2 teaspoons vegetable oil
**1 large (200g) brown onion,
    chopped coarsely**
2 cloves garlic, crushed
500g minced beef
2 tablespoons tomato sauce
2 tablespoons Worcestershire sauce
1 tablespoon barbecue sauce
1 beef stock cube
1 cup (250ml) water
1 cup (165g) cooked corn kernels
**1 cup (180g) coarsely chopped
    cooked potatoes**
**1 cup (160g) coarsely chopped
    cooked pumpkin**
**1/2 cup (100g) coarsely chopped
    cooked carrot**
**1/4 cup (30g) coarsely grated
    cheddar cheese**

TOPPING

**1 large (300g) potato,
    chopped coarsely**
300g pumpkin, chopped coarsely
40g butter
**1/4 cup (30g) coarsely grated
    cheddar cheese**

Heat oil in large pan; cook onion and garlic, stirring, until onion is soft. Add beef; cook, stirring, until well browned. Stir in combined sauces, stock cube and the water; bring to boil. Simmer, covered, 20 minutes. Add combined corn, potato, pumpkin and carrot; mix well. *[Can be made ahead to this stage. Cover; refrigerate overnight.]*

Spoon beef mixture into shallow 2-litre (8-cup capacity) oiled ovenproof baking dish. Spread Topping over beef mixture; sprinkle with the cheese. Bake, uncovered, in moderately hot oven about 30 minutes or until browned and hot.

Topping Boil, steam or microwave potato and pumpkin until tender; drain. Place potato and pumpkin in medium pan; mash over low heat until smooth. Stir in butter and cheese; cook, stirring, until butter and cheese melt and mixture is smooth.

SERVES 4

Far left Beef and black-bean stir-fry
Left Bubble and squeak pie
Above Oxtail with crispy bacon

SLOW-COOKED PORK WITH APPLES AND SAGE

1.4kg piece pork neck
1 tablespoon vegetable oil
2 large (300g) brown onions,
   chopped coarsely
2 cloves garlic, crushed
2 tablespoons honey
2 tablespoons Worcestershire sauce
2 tablespoons barbecue sauce
1/4 cup (60ml) dry white wine
3 medium (450g) apples,
   sliced thickly
1/2 cup (125ml) water
1/2 cup (125ml) cream
1/2 teaspoon ground nutmeg
1 teaspoon finely chopped fresh
   sage leaves

Tie kitchen string around whole piece pork neck at 2cm intervals.

Heat oil in large heavy-base flame-proof baking dish; cook onion and garlic, stirring, until onion is soft. Place pork on top of onion mixture in dish; brush with combined honey, Worcestershire and barbecue sauces. Cook, uncovered, in slow oven, brushing occasionally with sauce mixture, about 2 hours or until pork is tender. Remove pork from baking dish; cover to keep warm. Add wine to baking dish; cook, stirring, until reduced by half. Add all the remaining ingredients; cook, stirring, about 5 minutes or until apple is tender and sauce thickens. Slice pork; serve with apple mixture.

SERVES 4

MEDITERRANEAN LAMB WITH ROAST VEGETABLES

1kg butterflied boned
   lamb shoulder
100g butter, softened
1/2 teaspoon finely grated
   lemon rind
2 tablespoons finely chopped
   fresh parsley
2 teaspoons finely chopped
   fresh thyme
2 cloves garlic, crushed
1 tablespoon olive oil
4 small (320g) brown
   onions, quartered
2 medium (240g) zucchini,
   quartered
2 medium (160g) baby
   eggplants, quartered
1 medium (200g) red capsicum,
   sliced thickly
4 medium (800g) potatoes,
   quartered

HOMEMADE SAUSAGE ROLLS

- 2 large (600g) potatoes, quartered
- 2 teaspoons vegetable oil
- 1 large (200g) brown onion, grated coarsely
- 2 cloves garlic, crushed
- 1 teaspoon ground cumin
- 1 teaspoon curry powder
- 300g sausage mince
- 200g minced beef
- 4 sheets ready-rolled puff pastry
- 1 egg, beaten lightly

Boil, steam or microwave potato until just tender; drain, mash in medium bowl.

Heat oil in small pan; cook onion, garlic and spices, stirring, until onion is soft and liquid has evaporated. Combine onion mixture in large bowl with potato and minces; mix well.

Cut each pastry sheet in half; divide the mince mixture among pastry halves. Shape mince mixture down one long side of pastry; brush around edges with egg, roll to enclose filling. Cut rolls in half; brush with egg, score top of each roll with sharp knife. Place rolls, seam-side down, on oiled oven trays. *[Can be made ahead to this stage. Cover; refrigerate overnight or freeze.]* Bake, uncovered, in hot oven about 25 minutes or until browned.

MAKES 16

Far left Slow-cooked pork with apples and sage
Left Homemade sausage rolls
Below Mediterranean lamb with roast vegetables

Open lamb out flat; place, fat-side down, on board. Using a meat mallet, pound lamb to even thickness. Combine butter, rind, parsley, thyme and garlic in small bowl; spread mixture over fat-side of lamb. Place lamb in large shallow dish, cover; refrigerate 3 hours or overnight. *[Must be made ahead to this stage. Cover; freeze, if desired.]*

Heat oil in large heavy-base baking dish; cook lamb, uncovered, for about 2 minutes each side or until browned, remove from dish. Add onion, zucchini, eggplant, capsicum and potato; cook, stirring, until the vegetables are browned lightly. Place lamb, fat-side up, on top of the vegetables. Cook, uncovered, in moderately hot oven about 30 minutes or until lamb is cooked as desired. Remove lamb from dish; cover with foil to keep warm. Drain and discard excess pan juices, return vegetables to oven; bake, uncovered, in very hot oven about 10 minutes or until browned.

SERVES 4

PASTITSIO

We used ziti in this recipe but any long, tubular macaroni can be substituted.

1 tablespoon olive oil
1 medium (150g) brown onion, chopped coarsely
2 cloves garlic, crushed
500g minced lamb
400g can tomatoes
2 tablespoons tomato paste
1/4 cup (60ml) dry red wine
1/2 cup (125ml) beef stock
2 teaspoons dried oregano
1/2 teaspoon cracked black pepper
1/2 teaspoon ground cinnamon
1/2 teaspoon sweet paprika
250g ziti pasta
1/4 cup (20g) finely grated parmesan cheese
2 eggs, beaten lightly

SAUCE
80g butter
1/2 cup (75g) plain flour
2 cups (500ml) milk
1 cup (250ml) water
1/2 cup (40g) finely grated parmesan cheese
2 egg yolks

Heat oil in large pan; cook onion and garlic, stirring, until onion is soft. Add lamb; cook, stirring, until well browned. Stir in undrained crushed tomatoes, paste, wine, stock, oregano, pepper, cinnamon and paprika; bring mixture to boil. Simmer, uncovered, about 20 minutes or until mixture starts to thicken. [Can be made ahead to this stage. Cover; refrigerate overnight or freeze.]

Meanwhile, cook pasta in large pan of boiling water, uncovered, until just tender; drain, cool. Combine pasta, parmesan and eggs in medium bowl; mix well. Spread pasta mixture over base of oiled deep 3-litre (12-cup capacity) ovenproof dish.

Top with lamb mixture; pour Sauce over the top. [Can be made ahead to this stage. Cover; refrigerate overnight or freeze.] Bake, uncovered, in moderate oven about 45 minutes or until browned lightly and hot.

Sauce Heat butter in large pan; cook flour, stirring, until mixture thickens and bubbles. Gradually stir in combined milk and water; stir until sauce boils and thickens. Cool 10 minutes then stir in combined cheese and egg yolks.

SERVES 4

CHILLI CON CARNE PIE

1 tablespoon vegetable oil
1 large (200g) brown onion, chopped coarsely
2 cloves garlic, crushed
2 teaspoons ground cumin
1 tablespoon Mexican Chilli Powder
1kg minced beef
400g can tomatoes
1/4 cup (60ml) tomato paste
1 cup (250ml) water
420g can kidney beans, drained
3/4 cup (180ml) sour cream

PASTRY

2 cups (300g) plain flour
150g butter, chopped
¼ cup (30g) coarsely grated cheddar cheese
2 tablespoons finely chopped chives
1 egg yolk
2 tablespoons cold water
1 egg, beaten lightly

Heat oil in large pan; cook onion and garlic, stirring, until onion is soft. Add cumin and Chilli Powder; cook, stirring, until fragrant. Add beef; cook, stirring, until well browned. Add the undrained crushed tomatoes, paste, water and beans; simmer, uncovered, about 30 minutes or until mixture thickens, cool. *[Can be made ahead to this stage. Cover; refrigerate overnight or freeze.]* Pour beef mixture into pastry case then top with pastry shapes. Bake, uncovered, in moderate oven for about 15 minutes or until heated through. Serve pie with sour cream.

Pastry Grease 2-litre (8-cup capacity) ovenproof dish. Process flour and butter until just crumbly; add cheese, chives, egg yolk and enough water to make ingredients just cling together. Knead dough on floured surface until smooth, cover with plastic wrap; refrigerate at least 30 minutes.

Reserve a quarter of pastry; cover with plastic wrap. Roll remaining pastry on floured surface until large enough to line prepared dish. Lift pastry into dish, ease into side; trim edges. Cover; refrigerate at least 30 minutes.

Roll reserved pastry on floured surface until of a 5mm thickness; cut out shapes with cutter. Place pastry shapes on greased oven tray, cover; refrigerate at least 30 minutes.

Cover pastry-lined dish with baking paper; fill with dried beans or rice. Place on oven tray; bake, uncovered, in moderately hot oven 10 minutes. Remove and discard paper and beans, return dish to oven; bake, uncovered, 10 minutes or until browned lightly, cool.

Brush pastry shapes with egg; bake in moderately hot oven, uncovered, about 10 minutes or until browned lightly.

SERVES 4 TO 6

Far left Pastitsio
Above Chilli con carne pie

HONEY MUSTARD PORK CHOPS AND VEGETABLES

8 (1.5kg) pork loin chops
1/3 cup (80ml) honey
1 tablespoon Dijon mustard
1/2 teaspoon finely grated
   orange rind
1/4 cup (60ml) dry white wine
1 tablespoon vegetable oil
50g butter
2 cloves garlic, crushed
2 large (1kg) kumara,
   chopped coarsely
2 medium (240g) carrots,
   chopped coarsely
6 green onions, chopped coarsely

Combine pork in large shallow dish with honey, mustard, rind and wine. Cover; refrigerate 2 hours or overnight. *[Must be made ahead to this stage. Cover; freeze if desired.]* Drain chops from marinade; reserve marinade.

Heat oil in large pan; cook pork, in batches, brushing occasionally with reserved marinade, until browned both sides and cooked through. Discard any remaining marinade.

Meanwhile, combine melted butter, garlic, kumara, carrot and onion in large baking dish. Bake, uncovered, in moderately hot oven about 45 minutes or until vegetables are tender. Serve pork with baked vegetables.

SERVES 4

BACON, EGG AND CHEESE PIE

- **1¹/₂ cups (240g) wholemeal plain flour**
- **³/₄ cup (110g) plain flour**
- **185g butter, chopped coarsely**
- **3 egg yolks**
- **¹/₄ cup (60ml) iced water**
- **1 clove garlic, crushed**
- **1 large (200g) brown onion, chopped coarsely**
- **5 bacon rashers, chopped coarsely**
- **¹/₄ cup finely chopped fresh parsley**
- **3 eggs, beaten lightly**
- **1 cup (250ml) cream**
- **²/₃ cup (80g) coarsely grated smoked cheddar cheese**
- **6 eggs, extra**

Blend or process flours and butter until combined; add egg yolks and the water, process until ingredients just come together. Knead mixture on floured surface until smooth, wrap pastry in plastic wrap; refrigerate 30 minutes.

Roll ³/₄ of pastry between sheets of baking paper until large enough to line base and side of oiled 20cm springform tin. Lift pastry into tin, ease into side; trim edges. Lightly prick pastry base with fork, cover; refrigerate 30 minutes.

Cover pastry with baking paper; fill with dried beans or rice. Place tin on oven tray; bake, uncovered, in moderately hot oven 10 minutes. Remove and discard beans and paper; return tin to oven, bake, uncovered, 10 minutes or until browned lightly, cool.

Meanwhile, cook garlic, onion and bacon in large heated non-stick pan, stirring, until onion is soft and bacon is browned lightly. Cool bacon mixture; stir in parsley, eggs, cream and cheese, mix well. Pour a third of bacon mixture into cooled pastry case. Gently break 2 of the extra eggs into pastry case, taking care not to break the yolks. Repeat layering with remaining bacon mixture and extra eggs. Roll remaining pastry between sheets of baking paper until large enough to cover top of tin. Cover filling with pastry; brush edges with water, press around edges lightly with fork to seal. Bake pie, uncovered, in moderate oven about 1 hour or until top is browned and filling set.

SERVES 4 TO 6

Top left Bacon, egg and cheese pie
Left Honey mustard pork chops and vegetables
Right Silverbeet rissoles with quick tomato relish

SILVERBEET RISSOLES WITH QUICK TOMATO RELISH

- **¹/₂ cup (80g) burghul**
- **1kg silverbeet, trimmed**
- **750g minced beef**
- **1 medium (150g) brown onion, chopped finely**
- **1 clove garlic, crushed**
- **1 tablespoon Cajun Seasoning**

TOMATO RELISH
- **2 teaspoons vegetable oil**
- **1 small (80g) brown onion, chopped finely**
- **415g can tomatoes**
- **130g can corn kernels, drained**
- **¹/₄ cup (50g) firmly packed brown sugar**
- **¹/₄ cup (60ml) white vinegar**

Cover burghul with cold water; stand 30 minutes, drain.

Boil, steam or microwave silverbeet until just wilted; drain. Squeeze excess liquid from silverbeet; chop roughly.

Using hand, combine burghul and silverbeet in large bowl with beef, onion, garlic and Seasoning. Form mixture into 12 rissole shapes; place on tray. *[Can be made ahead to this stage. Cover; refrigerate overnight or freeze.]*

Cook rissoles, in batches, in large heated oiled non-stick pan until browned both sides and cooked through. Serve rissoles with Tomato Relish.

Tomato Relish Heat oil in medium pan; cook onion, stirring, until soft. Add undrained crushed tomatoes, corn, sugar and vinegar; stir over low heat until sugar dissolves. Bring to boil; simmer, uncovered, stirring occasionally, about 25 minutes or until relish thickens. *[Can be made a day ahead. Cover; refrigerate overnight or freeze.]*

SERVES 4

SAUSAGE RISOTTO

500g beef sausages

4 small (520g) tomatoes

2 tablespoons olive oil

1 large (500g) leek,
   chopped coarsely

1 clove garlic, crushed

1/4 cup (60ml) dry red wine

2 cups (400g) calrose rice

2 litres (8 cups) boiling water

2 tablespoons beef stock powder

1/2 cup (40g) finely grated
   parmesan cheese

1 tablespoon finely chopped
   fresh parsley

Cook sausages in heated oiled pan until browned all over and cooked through; slice thickly.

Cut tomatoes into wedges; place wedges on oven tray, brush with half the oil. Bake tomato in moderate oven about 15 minutes or until softened.

Heat remaining oil in large pan; cook leek and garlic, stirring, until leek is soft. Add wine; simmer until liquid is reduced by half. Stir in rice, and blended water and stock powder; simmer, uncovered, stirring occasionally, about 25 minutes or until most of liquid is absorbed and rice is just tender. Just before serving, stir in sausages, tomato, cheese and parsley.

SERVES 4

LAMB SAUSAGES WITH PUMPKIN-POTATO MASH

2 teaspoons vegetable oil

1 small (80g) brown onion,
   chopped finely

1 clove garlic, crushed

1 1/2 tablespoons mild curry paste

750g minced lamb

1 tablespoon finely chopped
   fresh parsley

1 egg, beaten lightly

1 cup (70g) stale breadcrumbs

600g piece pumpkin,
   coarsely chopped

3 medium (600g) potatoes,
   chopped coarsely

1 tablespoon milk

1/2 cup (60g) coarsely grated
   cheddar cheese

Heat oil in small pan; cook onion, garlic and paste, stirring, until onion is soft. Using hand, combine onion mixture, lamb, half the parsley, egg and bread-crumbs in large bowl; mix well. Shape 1/4 cups of mixture into sausages. Cover; refrigerate 1 hour or until firm. [Can be made ahead to this stage. Cover; refrigerate overnight or freeze.] Cook sausages in large oiled pan, in batches, until browned all over and cooked through. Meanwhile, boil, steam or microwave pumpkin and potato, separately, until tender; drain. Mash pumpkin and potato in large bowl with milk and cheese. Serve sausages with mash, sprinkled with remaining parsley.

SERVES 4

GLAZED MOCK HAM

2kg corned leg of lamb
1 cup (250ml) white vinegar
1/2 cup (100g) brown sugar
2 bay leaves
1 teaspoon whole black peppercorns
1 medium (150g) onion,
    chopped finely

REDCURRANT LEMON GLAZE
1 medium (140g) lemon
3/4 cup (250g) redcurrant jelly

Combine all ingredients in large pan, add enough water to just cover lamb; bring to boil. Simmer, covered, 1 hour.

Remove lamb from pan; discard liquid. Place lamb on wire rack in large shallow baking dish; brush with half the Redcurrant Lemon Glaze. Bake, uncovered, in moderate oven, brushing occasionally with remaining glaze, about 1 1/4 hours or until lamb is tender.

Redcurrant Lemon Glaze Using vegetable peeler, slice rind thinly from lemon; cut rind into thin strips. Place the rind in a small pan of boiling water; boil, uncovered, for 2 minutes; drain. Squeeze juice from lemon (you need 2 tablespoons), combine with rind and jelly in the same pan; cook, stirring, until jelly melts.

SERVES 4

Far left Sausage risotto
Left Glazed mock ham
Above Lamb sausages with pumpkin-potato mash

MEATBALLS, RATATOUILLE AND RICOTTA RICE CAKE

500g minced beef
1 small (80g) brown onion,
chopped finely
2 cloves garlic, crushed
1 tablespoon tomato paste
1 teaspoon ground coriander
1/2 cup (35g) stale breadcrumbs
1/2 teaspoon finely grated
lemon rind
2 tablespoons olive oil

RATATOUILLE

2 tablespoons olive oil
1 large (200g) brown onion,
sliced thickly
2 cloves garlic, crushed
1 medium (200g) green capsicum,
chopped coarsely
1 medium (120g) zucchini,
chopped coarsely
1 (80g) finger eggplant,
chopped coarsely

2 tablespoons tomato paste
400g can tomatoes
1/2 cup (125ml) vegetable stock

RICOTTA RICE CAKE

1 tablespoon polenta
2 cups (400g) ricotta cheese
1/4 cup (20g) finely grated
parmesan cheese
1/2 cup (110g) cooked
long-grain rice
1 egg, separated
1 tablespoon finely shredded
fresh basil leaves

Combine beef, onion, garlic, paste, coriander, breadcrumbs and rind in large bowl; mix well. Using floured hands, roll level tablespoons of beef mixture into balls; place on tray. *[Can be made ahead to this stage. Cover; refrigerate overnight or freeze.]*

Heat oil in large pan; cook meatballs, in batches, until browned all over and cooked through, drain on absorbent paper. Serve Meatballs with Ratatouille and Ricotta Rice Cake.

Ratatouille Heat oil in large pan; cook onion and garlic, stirring, until onion is soft. Add capsicum, zucchini and eggplant; cook, stirring, until vegetables are soft. Add paste, undrained crushed tomatoes and stock; simmer, uncovered, about 10 minutes or until sauce thickens.

Ricotta Rice Cake Oil base of 20cm round sandwich cake pan; line base with foil, grease foil. Sprinkle polenta over base and side of prepared pan.

Combine ricotta, parmesan, rice, egg yolk and basil in large bowl; mix well. Whisk egg white in small bowl until soft peaks form; fold egg white through cheese mixture. Spread into prepared pan; bake, uncovered, in moderately hot oven about 30 minutes or until firm. Cool 5 minutes before cutting into wedges.

SERVES 4

Above Meatballs, ratatouille and ricotta rice cake
Right Glazed corned silverside with vegetable gratin

GLAZED CORNED SILVERSIDE WITH VEGETABLE GRATIN

*We used an eye piece of silverside
for this recipe.*

1.5kg corned beef silverside
6 black peppercorns
1 bay leaf
1 large (200g) brown onion, halved
**1 medium (120g) carrot,
   chopped coarsely**
1 tablespoon malt vinegar
**1/4 cup (50g) firmly packed
   brown sugar**
2 tablespoons marmalade
1 tablespoon sweet chilli sauce
2 teaspoons soy sauce
1 clove garlic, crushed

VEGETABLE GRATIN
300g cauliflower florets
300g broccoli florets
**1 large (180g) carrot,
   chopped coarsely**
1/2 cup (60g) frozen peas
40g butter
**1 medium (350g) leek,
   chopped coarsely**
2 tablespoons plain flour
2 cups (500ml) milk
**3/4 cup (90g) coarsely grated
   cheddar cheese**

Combine silverside, peppercorns, bay leaf, onion, carrot, vinegar and sugar in large pan; add enough water to just cover silverside. Bring to boil; simmer, covered, about 2 hours or until silverside is tender. Cool silverside in liquid in pan for 1 hour. Remove silverside from pan; discard liquid. *[Can be made ahead to this stage. Cover; refrigerate.]*

Place silverside on oiled oven tray; brush all over with combined remaining ingredients. Bake, uncovered, in moderate oven about 25 minutes or until silverside is browned and heated through. Drizzle silverside with pan juices and serve with Vegetable Gratin.

Vegetable Gratin   Boil, steam or microwave cauliflower, broccoli and carrot until just tender; drain. Place in greased 1.5-litre (6-cup capacity) oven-proof dish; sprinkle peas over vegetables. Melt butter in small pan; cook leek, stirring, until soft. Add flour; cook, stirring, until mixture thickens and bubbles. Gradually stir in milk; stir until mixture boils and thickens. Stir in cheese; pour sauce over vegetables. *[Can be made ahead to this stage. Cover; refrigerate overnight.]* Bake gratin, uncovered, in moderate oven about 25 minutes or until browned.

SERVES 4

SANG CHOY BOW

The fried noodles used here are called crunchy dried noodles and are sold in 100g cellophane bags.

1 tablespoon vegetable oil
1 medium (150g) brown onion, chopped finely
1 clove garlic, crushed
600g pork and veal mince
1 tablespoon soy sauce
1 tablespoon oyster sauce
250g bean sprouts
200g fried noodles
3 green onions, sliced thinly
8 large lettuce leaves
1 tablespoon sesame seeds, toasted

Heat oil in large pan; cook brown onion and garlic, stirring, until onion is soft. Add mince; cook, stirring, until mince is well browned. Add combined sauces; simmer, uncovered, stirring occasionally, 5 minutes. Just before serving, stir in sprouts, noodles and green onion. Divide mince mixture among lettuce leaves, sprinkle with sesame seeds.

SERVES 4

GLAZED PICKLED PORK

2.5kg hand of pickled pork
2 medium (300g) brown onions, quartered
6 cloves
4 bay leaves
$1/2$ teaspoon black peppercorns
$1/2$ cup (60ml) cider vinegar
$1/2$ cup (100g) firmly packed brown sugar
2 medium (300g) apples
1 bunch (400g) baby carrots, trimmed
$1/4$ cup (60ml) apple juice

Combine pork, onion, cloves, bay leaves, peppercorns, vinegar and half the sugar in large pan; add enough water to just cover pork, bring to boil. Simmer, covered, about 2 hours or until pork is tender. Cool pork in liquid for 1 hour.

Quarter unpeeled apples, remove and discard cores; cut apple quarters into thick slices. Remove pork from pan; discard liquid. Place the pork in shallow oiled baking dish with apples and carrots; brush pork with combined remaining sugar and juice. Bake, uncovered, in moderate oven, brushing occasionally with sugar and juice, about 30 minutes or until pork is browned. Serve pork with apples and carrots.

SERVES 4 TO 6

BEEF AND BEAN STEW WITH POLENTA WEDGES

2 teaspoons olive oil

1 small (80g) brown onion, chopped finely

1 clove garlic, crushed

300g minced beef

2 x 420g cans soya beans, rinsed, drained

1/4 cup (60ml) tomato paste

1 tablespoon Worcestershire sauce

2 teaspoons mild chilli sauce

2 tablespoons barbecue sauce

2 cups (500ml) beef stock

2 tablespoons finely chopped fresh parsley

1/3 cup (80ml) sour cream

POLENTA WEDGES

1 tablespoon olive oil

1 medium (150g) brown onion, sliced thinly

3 cups (750ml) beef stock

1 1/2 cups (250g) polenta

1/2 cup (60g) coarsely grated cheddar cheese

Heat oil in large pan; cook onion and garlic, stirring, until onion is soft. Add beef; cook, stirring, until browned. Stir in beans, paste, sauces and stock; simmer, uncovered, stirring occasionally, about 20 minutes or until mixture thickens. *[Can be made ahead. Cover; refrigerate overnight or freeze.]* Stir in parsley just before serving. Serve stew with Polenta Wedges and sour cream.

Polenta Wedges Grease a 20cm x 30cm lamington pan; line base with baking paper. Heat oil in large pan; cook onion, stirring, about 5 minutes or until just browned; remove from pan. Bring stock to boil in the same pan. Gradually stir in polenta; simmer, stirring, about 5 minutes or until mixture thickens. Stir in cheese and reserved onion. Press polenta mixture into prepared pan, cover; refrigerate until firm. *[Can be made ahead to this stage. Cover; refrigerate overnight or freeze.]*

Just before serving, turn polenta onto board. Cut polenta in half lengthways; cut each half into three 10cm squares, then cut each square into triangles. Cook polenta wedges, in batches, in large heated oiled pan until browned both sides.

SERVES 4

Left Sang choy bow
Above left Glazed pickled pork
Above Beef and bean stew with polenta wedges

MEATLOAF ITALIAN-STYLE

1kg minced beef
**1 small (80g) brown onion,
   chopped finely**
2 cloves garlic, crushed
1/4 cup (60ml) tomato paste
**1/4 cup (40g) coarsely chopped
   black olives**
1 teaspoon dried oregano
**1 tablespoon finely chopped
   fresh parsley**
**1/4 cup (20g) finely grated
   parmesan cheese**
1 cup (70g) stale breadcrumbs
1 egg
1/4 cup (60ml) tomato sauce
2 teaspoons Worcestershire sauce

TOMATO GRAVY

2 teaspoons olive oil
**1 small (80g) brown onion,
   chopped finely**
415g can tomatoes
1 tablespoon gravy mix
1/2 cup (125ml) water

STIR-FRIED PASTA, TOMATO AND CHILLI PORK

*We used bucatini in this recipe but use any
length pasta you like – try penne or rigatoni.*

375g bucatini pasta
1 tablespoon olive oil
**1 medium (150g) brown onion,
   chopped coarsely**
2 cloves garlic, crushed
1 bird's-eye chilli, sliced finely
500g minced pork
1 teaspoon mixed spice
1/2 teaspoon ground cinnamon
**2 tablespoons finely chopped
   fresh parsley**
**2 tablespoons finely shredded
   fresh mint leaves**
**4 medium (760g) tomatoes,
   seeded, sliced thinly**
1 cup (250ml) yogurt

Cook pasta in large pan of boiling water,
uncovered, until just tender; drain, cover
to keep warm.

Meanwhile, heat oil in wok or large
pan; stir-fry onion, garlic and chilli until
onion is soft. Add pork, mixed spice and
cinnamon; stir-fry until pork is well
browned. Add parsley, mint, tomato and
pasta; stir-fry until hot. Serve pasta
mixture topped with yogurt.

SERVES 4

Above Stir-fried pasta, tomato and chilli pork
Right Meatloaf Italian-style
Far right Rosti-topped sausages and
garlicky cabbage

Combine beef, onion, garlic, paste, olives, herbs, cheese, breadcrumbs and egg in large bowl; mix well. Press mixture into 14cm x 21cm loaf pan.

Bake, uncovered, in moderate oven 45 minutes. Brush top of meatloaf with combined sauces; bake, uncovered, about 30 minutes or until cooked through. Drain juices from pan; stand 5 minutes before slicing. [Can be made a day ahead. Cover; refrigerate overnight.] Serve meatloaf with Tomato Gravy.

Tomato Gravy Heat oil in small pan; cook onion, stirring, until soft. Add undrained crushed tomatoes and blended gravy mix and water; simmer, stirring, until thickened. [Can be made a day ahead. Cover; refrigerate overnight.]

SERVES 4

ROSTI-TOPPED SAUSAGES AND GARLICKY CABBAGE

1kg thick beef sausages
1 medium (150g) brown onion, chopped coarsely
1 clove garlic, crushed
400g can tomatoes
1 cup (250ml) water
2 tablespoons tomato paste
$1/2$ teaspoon dried basil
2 tablespoons finely chopped fresh parsley
$1/2$ teaspoon sweet paprika

ROSTI TOPPING
1kg potatoes
1 cup (125g) coarsely grated cheddar cheese

GARLICKY CABBAGE
30g butter
$1/2$ medium (750g) cabbage, chopped coarsely
1 clove garlic, crushed
2 tablespoons dry white wine
2 tablespoons finely chopped fresh chives

Cook sausages in large heated pan, in batches, until browned all over. Drain on absorbent paper; slice thickly. Discard fat in pan; cook onion and garlic, stirring, until onion is soft. Return sausages to pan with undrained crushed tomatoes, the water, paste, basil and parsley, bring to the boil; simmer, uncovered, about 10 minutes or until mixture thickens. Place sausage mixture in shallow 3-litre (12-cup capacity) ovenproof dish. [Can be made ahead to this stage. Cover; refrigerate overnight or freeze.] Cover sausage mixture with Rosti Topping, sprinkle with paprika; bake in moderately hot oven about 30 minutes or until browned. Serve with Garlicky Cabbage.

Rosti Topping Boil, steam or microwave potatoes until just tender; drain, cool. Coarsely grate potato into large bowl, combine with cheese.

Garlicky Cabbage Melt butter in large pan; cook cabbage, garlic and wine, stirring, until cabbage is just tender. Just before serving, stir in chives.

SERVES 4

LAMB SHANKS WITH SPICED KUMARA AND PUMPKIN

2 teaspoons caraway seeds
1 tablespoon ground cumin
1 tablespoon ground coriander
2 cloves garlic, crushed
1/4 cup (60ml) olive oil
8 lamb shanks, trimmed
1 medium (150g) brown onion, chopped coarsely
2 medium (240g) carrots, chopped coarsely
4 trimmed (300g) sticks celery, chopped coarsely
1 medium (125g) parsnip, chopped coarsely
1 medium (350g) leek, chopped coarsely
1 tablespoon olive oil, extra
1 cup (250ml) dry red wine
1 1/2 cups (375ml) beef stock
400g can tomatoes
1 tablespoon tomato puree
1 teaspoon sugar

SPICED KUMARA AND PUMPKIN
1 medium (400g) kumara, chopped coarsely
400g pumpkin, chopped coarsely
2 teaspoons ground nutmeg
2 teaspoons ground cumin
2 tablespoons olive oil

Place caraway seeds in small heated dry pan; cook, stirring, until fragrant. Combine caraway in large bowl with cumin, coriander, garlic and oil; mix well. Place lamb in bowl; rub spice mixture over lamb. Cover; refrigerate 3 hours or overnight. [Best made ahead to this stage. Cover; refrigerate overnight or freeze.]

Combine the onion, carrot, celery, parsnip, leek and extra oil in large baking dish; mix well. Bake, uncovered, in hot oven about 10 minutes or until vegetables are browned lightly. Place lamb on top vegetables; pour combined wine, stock, undrained crushed tomatoes and puree over the top. Bake, uncovered, in slow oven, turning occasionally, about 3 hours or until lamb is tender. Remove lamb from dish; cover to keep warm. Blend or process vegetables and liquid until almost smooth; strain into medium pan. Stir in sugar; boil about 2 minutes or until sauce thickens. Serve lamb with Spiced Kumara and Pumpkin, drizzle with sauce.

Spiced Kumara and Pumpkin Combine all ingredients in medium baking dish; bake, uncovered, in hot oven about 25 minutes or until tender.

SERVES 4

BEEF POT ROAST WITH POTATO TIMBALES

Use only pouring cream for this recipe.

2 tablespoons vegetable oil
2kg beef blade roast
**2 medium (300g) brown onions,
    sliced thinly**
2 cloves garlic, crushed
**1/4 cup finely chopped
    fresh oregano leaves**
**8 medium (1.5kg) tomatoes,
    chopped coarsely**
400g can tomatoes
1/2 cup (125ml) dry red wine
2 bay leaves
1 tablespoon soy sauce
1 tablespoon Worcestershire sauce
2 tablespoons brown sugar

POTATO TIMBALES
2 eggs
300ml cream
1 teaspoon ground nutmeg
1 clove garlic, crushed
**2 medium (400g) potatoes,
    sliced thinly**
**1 medium (150g) white onion,
    chopped finely**

Heat half the oil in large pan; cook beef until browned all over, remove from pan. Heat remaining oil in pan; cook onion and garlic, stirring, until onion is soft. Add oregano and fresh tomato; cook, stirring, about 3 minutes or until tomato is soft. Return beef to pan with any juices, undrained crushed tomatoes and remaining ingredients; simmer, covered, turning occasionally, about 3 hours or until beef is tender.

Remove beef from pan; cover to keep warm. Simmer sauce, uncovered, about 10 minutes or until thickened slightly. Serve thinly sliced beef with sauce and Potato Timbales.

Potatoes Timbales Grease four 1-cup (250ml-capacity) ovenproof dishes. Whisk eggs, cream, nutmeg and garlic in medium bowl. Layer potato and onion among prepared dishes; pour over egg mixture. Cover each dish with foil, place on oven tray; bake in moderate oven about 25 minutes or until potato is tender. Remove foil; bake potato about 5 minutes or until browned.

SERVES 4

Left Lamb shanks with spiced kumara
and pumpkin
Right Beef pot roast with potato timbales

BOMBAY LAMB WITH LENTILS AND BANANA RAITA

3 teaspoons ground cumin
1¹/2 teaspoons ground aniseed
1/2 teaspoon ground chilli
1 teaspoon ground turmeric
2 teaspoons ground ginger
1 teaspoon ground cinnamon
1/4 cup (60ml) vegetable oil
8 (1kg) lamb loin chops
1 cup (200g) red lentils, rinsed
2 cups (500ml) chicken stock
1 clove garlic, crushed

BANANA RAITA
30g butter
3 teaspoons brown sugar
2 medium (400g) bananas,
  sliced thickly
1¹/2 cups (375ml) yogurt

MINCED BEEF AND CRACKED WHEAT LASAGNE

Cracked wheat is the whole unprocessed wheat berry broken into fragments. We used a medium grind in this recipe.

1 tablespoon olive oil
1 large (200g) brown onion,
  chopped coarsely
2 cloves garlic, crushed
300g minced beef
2 x 415g cans tomatoes
1/4 cup (60ml) tomato paste
1/4 teaspoon mixed dried herbs
3 cups (750ml) water
1 cup (160g) cracked wheat
1/2 teaspoon ground nutmeg
250g instant lasagne sheets
2¹/2 cups (310g) coarsely grated
  cheddar cheese

Heat oil in large pan; cook onion and garlic, stirring, until onion is soft. Add beef; cook, stirring, until browned. Add undrained crushed tomatoes, paste, herbs, the water and wheat; simmer, uncovered, stirring occasionally, about 25 minutes or until wheat is tender. Stir in nutmeg.

Spread a third of the beef mixture over base of oiled shallow 2.5-litre (10-cup capacity) ovenproof dish; cover with a third of lasagne sheets and 1/4 cup of the cheese. Repeat layering with another third of the beef mixture, another third of lasagne sheets and another 1/4 cup cheese. Finish layering using remaining beef mixture, lasagne sheets and cheese. Cover with foil; bake in moderate oven 45 minutes. *[Can be made ahead to this stage. Cover; refrigerate up to 2 days or freeze.]* Remove foil; bake, uncovered, about 15 minutes or until browned on top. Stand 10 minutes before serving.

SERVES 4

Combine spices and oil in large bowl, add lamb; mix well. Cover; refrigerate 3 hours or overnight. *[Must be made ahead to this stage. Cover; refrigerate or freeze.]*

Combine lentils, stock and garlic in medium pan, bring to boil; simmer, uncovered, about 10 minutes or until lentils are just tender.

Cook lamb, in batches, in large heated oiled pan until browned both sides and cooked as desired. Serve lamb and lentils with Banana Raita.

Banana Raita Melt butter and sugar in medium heated pan; cook banana slices until browned lightly and soft. Combine banana with yogurt in medium bowl.

SERVES 4

SLOPPY JOES AND COLESLAW

No one knows the origin of the name, but this American version of savoury mince is everybody's favourite.

1 tablespoon vegetable oil
2 medium (340g) brown onions, chopped finely
1 small (150g) green capsicum, chopped finely
1 trimmed (75g) celery stick, chopped finely
750g minced beef
2 tablespoons American mustard
1 tablespoon dark brown sugar
2 tablespoons cider vinegar
1 cup (250ml) tomato ketchup
6 hamburger buns
3 kosher dill pickles, sliced thinly

COLESLAW
1 medium (200g) red capsicum, chopped finely
2 trimmed (150g) celery sticks, chopped finely
3 green onions, sliced thinly
200g red cabbage, shredded finely
200g white cabbage, shredded finely
2 medium (240g) carrots, grated coarsely
1/2 cup (125ml) vegetable oil
1/2 cup (125ml) cider vinegar

2 teaspoons seeded mustard
2 teaspoons sugar
2 tablespoons finely chopped fresh parsley

Heat oil in large pan; cook onion, capsicum and celery, stirring, until onion is soft. Add beef; cook, stirring, until well browned. Stir in mustard, sugar, vinegar and ketchup; bring to boil. Simmer Sloppy Joe mixture, covered, about 40 minutes or until slightly thickened.

Halve buns, toast cut sides. Divide pickles among bun bases, top with Sloppy Joe and Coleslaw; cover with tops of buns. Serve remaining Coleslaw, separately as salad, if desired.

Coleslaw Combine capsicum, celery, onion, cabbages and carrot in large bowl. Just before serving, toss with combined remaining ingredients.

MAKES 6

Far left Minced beef and cracked wheat lasagne
Left Bombay lamb with lentils and banana raita
Above Sloppy Joes and coleslaw

BBQ RIBS WITH BAKED POTATO AND CORN SALAD

1.5kg American-style pork
   spare ribs
1/2 cup (125ml) plum sauce
1 tablespoon soy sauce
1 tablespoon sweet chilli sauce
1 clove garlic, crushed

BAKED POTATO AND CORN SALAD
4 medium (800g) potatoes
2 (500g) trimmed corn cobs
1 large (200g) brown onion,
   sliced thinly
2 trimmed (150g) celery sticks,
   sliced thinly
1 large (350g) red capsicum,
   sliced thinly
2 tablespoons mayonnaise
2 tablespoons lemon juice
2 tablespoons sour cream
1 tablespoon sweet chilli sauce
2 tablespoons finely chopped
   fresh parsley

Place ribs in large shallow dish; coat with combined sauces and garlic. Cover; refrigerate 3 hours or overnight. *[Must be made ahead to this stage. Cover; refrigerate or freeze.]*

Drain ribs; reserve marinade. Return ribs to same baking dish; bake, uncovered, in moderate oven, brushing with reserved marinade, for about 45 minutes or until browned and tender. Serve ribs with Baked Potato and Corn Salad.

Baked Potato and Corn Salad Wrap potatoes in foil; bake in moderate oven about 1 hour or until tender. Cool 15 minutes; cut potatoes into quarters. Boil, steam or microwave corn until just tender; drain, cut kernels from cob.

Combine potato, corn and onion in large bowl with celery and capsicum. Gently toss vegetables with combined remaining ingredients.

SERVES 4

MOROCCAN-STYLE LAMB WITH CORIANDER COUSCOUS

2 medium (600g) eggplants
coarse cooking salt
1 tablespoon olive oil
8 (1kg) lamb loin chops
2 medium (300g) brown onions,
   sliced thickly
2 teaspoons ground cumin
2 teaspoons ground coriander
1/4 teaspoon ground cinnamon
1 litre (4 cups) beef stock
4 medium (480g) zucchini,
   sliced thickly
1/4 cup (60ml) apricot jam

CORIANDER COUSCOUS
1 cup (250ml) water
2 cups (400g) couscous
40g butter
2 tablespoons finely chopped fresh
   coriander leaves

Cut eggplant into 1cm slices, place on wire rack, sprinkle with salt; allow to stand 30 minutes. Rinse slices under cold water; drain on absorbent paper, cut slices into quarters.

Heat oil in large pan; cook lamb, uncovered, until browned both sides, remove from pan. Add onion; cook, stirring, until soft. Add spices; cook, stirring, until fragrant. Return lamb and any juices to pan with stock; simmer, covered, about 1 hour or until lamb is just tender. Stir in eggplant, zucchini and jam; simmer, uncovered, about 30 minutes or until vegetables are tender. Serve lamb with Coriander Couscous.

Coriander Couscous Bring the water to boil in medium pan, gradually add couscous; remove from heat. Cover; stand about 5 minutes or until all water is absorbed. Stir in butter and coriander; fluff with fork.

SERVES 4

MELT-IN-THE-MOUTH LAMB SHOULDER

1.2kg lamb shoulder
2 tablespoons seeded mustard
2 cloves garlic, crushed
1/3 cup (80ml) dry red wine
2 2/3 cups (660ml) beef stock
12 ice cubes
1 tablespoon cornflour
1 tablespoon water
4 small (400g) red onions

Place lamb in large pan of boiling water; boil, uncovered, 15 minutes. Remove lamb from pan; discard cooking liquid. Place lamb in large oiled flameproof baking dish; using sharp knife, make 10 deep cuts across top of lamb. Rub combined mustard and garlic over lamb, pressing into cuts; pour stock over lamb.

Cover lamb with foil; bake in very slow oven 5 hours, turning lamb occasionally. Remove foil, add peeled whole onions; bake, uncovered, about 1 hour or until lamb is browned and onions are soft. Remove lamb and onions from pan; cover to keep warm. Add ice cubes to hot stock (this helps solidify the fat); remove fat with slotted spoon. Bring stock to boil; boil 5 minutes or until stock is reduced by half. Stir in blended cornflour and the water; cook until stock boils and thickens slightly. Serve lamb with sauce and roasted red onions.

SERVES 4

Left BBQ ribs with baked potato and corn salad
Top right Moroccan-style lamb with coriander couscous
Right Melt-in-the-mouth lamb shoulder

Rectangular plate from Orson & Blake Collectables

Chic & cheerful chicken

Of all meats, poultry is possibly the most versatile, easily available and acceptable to practically everyone. You'll find that the number of ways you can serve chicken is limited only by your imagination

GREEK-STYLE CHICKEN AND RISONI CASSEROLE

Substitute orzo for the risoni if you wish: both are small, almost rice-sized pastas.

2 tablespoons olive oil
2 cloves garlic, crushed
1.5kg chicken
1 medium (150g) brown onion, chopped coarsely
1 medium (200g) red capsicum, chopped coarsely
2 cups (500ml) chicken stock
2 x 400g cans tomatoes
2 teaspoons dried oregano
1/4 teaspoon ground sweet paprika
1 cup (220g) risoni pasta
2 bay leaves
1/4 cup (40g) seeded black olives

Combine oil and garlic in small bowl. Place chicken, breast-side up, in large oiled baking dish; brush with half the oil mixture. Bake, uncovered, in moderate oven 1 hour.

Meanwhile, in large pan, heat remaining oil mixture; cook onion and capsicum, stirring, until onion is soft, remove from heat. Combine stock, undrained crushed tomatoes, oregano, paprika, risoni and bay leaves in pan with onion mixture; pour around chicken in baking dish. Bake, uncovered, in moderate oven 30 minutes or until risoni is tender and chicken cooked through. *[Can be made ahead to this stage. Cover; refrigerate overnight.]*

Just before serving, sprinkle with olives; serve with stir-fried spinach, if desired.

SERVES 4

SAUSAGES, CARAMELISED ONIONS AND MASH

1kg minced chicken
1 clove garlic, crushed
1/4 cup finely chopped fresh parsley
1 egg
1 tablespoon ground cumin
1 cup (100g) packaged breadcrumbs
1/4 cup vegetable oil
4 large (360g) egg
    tomatoes, halved

CARAMELISED ONIONS

90g butter
4 large (800g) brown onions,
    sliced thinly
2 tablespoons malt vinegar
1/4 cup (50g) firmly packed
    brown sugar

MASH

6 large (1.8kg) potatoes,
    chopped coarsely
1/2 cup (125ml) hot milk
1 teaspoon salt

Using hand, combine chicken, garlic, parsley, egg and cumin in large bowl; roll half cups of mixture into sausage shapes, coat with breadcrumbs. Place sausages on tray, cover; refrigerate 2 hours. *[Can be prepared ahead to this stage. Cover; refrigerate overnight or freeze.]*

Heat oil in large pan; cook sausages, in batches, until browned all over and almost cooked through. Halve sausages lengthways; return to pan, cut-side down. Cook until browned and cooked through; drain on absorbent paper. Place tomato in same pan; cook, turning occasionally, until just browned. Serve sausages with tomato, Caramelised Onions and Mash.

Caramelised Onions Heat butter in large pan; cook onion, stirring, until soft. Add vinegar and sugar; cook, stirring, about 15 minutes or until the onion is soft and liquid is reduced.

Mash Boil, steam or microwave potatoes until tender; drain, mash in large bowl with milk and salt.

SERVES 4 TO 6

PENNE WITH CHICKEN LIVERS AND ROASTED TOMATOES

You can use any short pasta in this recipe.

3 cloves garlic, peeled
1 tablespoon olive oil
12 medium (900g) egg
    tomatoes, halved
1 cup (250ml) chicken stock
2 teaspoons sugar
500g penne
750g chicken livers
4 bacon rashers, chopped coarsely
1 medium (150g) brown onion,
    chopped finely
2 tablespoons finely chopped
    fresh rosemary

Combine garlic and oil in small bowl. Place tomato, cut-side up, in baking dish, drizzle with strained garlic oil; bake, uncovered, in very hot oven about 40 minutes or until soft. Blend or process tomato, in batches, with stock and sugar until almost smooth. *[Can be made ahead to this stage. Cover; refrigerate overnight or freeze.]*

Cook pasta in large pan of boiling water, uncovered, until just tender; drain.

Meanwhile, rinse livers under cold water, discarding any fat and membrane; cut in half. Cook bacon in large heated pan, stirring, until crisp and browned; drain excess fat from pan. Add onion, liver and rosemary; cook, stirring, until liver is browned and just cooked. Stir in tomato mixture, simmer 1 minute then add pasta; simmer, stirring, until hot. Top with a little extra chopped rosemary and parsley just before serving, if desired.

SERVES 4

MOROCCAN CHICKEN CASSEROLE

1 cup (200g) dried chickpeas
1.6kg chicken
1 tablespoon vegetable oil
2 medium (300g) brown onions,
**   sliced thickly**
2 cloves garlic, crushed
3 teaspoons ground cumin
3 teaspoons ground coriander
1 teaspoon ground turmeric
1 cinnamon stick
2 x 400g cans tomatoes
2 strips lemon peel
2 tablespoons lemon juice
1¹/₂ cups (375ml) chicken stock
2 tablespoons coarsely chopped
**   fresh coriander leaves**

Place chickpeas in medium bowl, cover with water; soak overnight. Drain chickpeas; rinse under cold water, drain.

Using a sharp knife or scissors, cut thigh and leg portions from chicken; separate legs and thighs. Cut wing portions from chicken. Cut along each side of backbone, discard backbone; cut breast section in half (you will have 8 pieces).

Heat oil in large pan; cook onion and garlic, stirring, until onion is soft. Add cumin, ground coriander and turmeric; cook, stirring, until fragrant. Add chicken, cook, stirring, until chicken is browned lightly. Add cinnamon stick, undrained crushed tomatoes, peel, juice, stock and chickpeas; bring to boil. Simmer, covered, 1 hour; uncover, simmer about 15 minutes or until chickpeas are tender and sauce is thickened. Just before serving, stir in fresh coriander. *[Can be made a day ahead. Cover; refrigerate overnight.]* Serve with steamed couscous, if desired.

SERVES 4

Left Sausages, caramelised onions
and mash
Top right Penne with chicken livers and
roasted tomatoes
Right Moroccan chicken casserole

SPINACH AND CHICKEN LASAGNE

2 teaspoons olive oil
1 medium (150g) brown onion, chopped coarsely
1 clove garlic, crushed
1kg minced chicken
2 x 415g cans diced tomatoes
2 tablespoons tomato paste
1 teaspoon dried oregano
1 teaspoon dried basil
500g spinach
60g butter
1/4 cup (35g) plain flour
2 cups (500ml) milk
1 cup (125g) coarsely grated cheddar cheese
175g instant lasagne sheets

Heat oil in large pan; cook onion and garlic, stirring, until onion is soft. Add chicken; cook, stirring, until chicken is changed in colour. Stir in undrained tomatoes, paste, oregano and basil; simmer, uncovered, stirring occasionally, about 30 minutes or until most of the liquid is absorbed.

Meanwhile, trim spinach; discard stems. Boil, steam or microwave spinach until just wilted; drain. Squeeze excess liquid from spinach; chop coarsely.

Melt butter in small pan. Add flour; cook, stirring, until mixture thickens and bubbles. Gradually stir in milk; stir until mixture boils and thickens. Remove from heat; stir in cheese and spinach.

Place a third of the lasagne sheets over base of oiled shallow 2-litre (8-cup capacity) ovenproof dish. Cover with half the chicken mixture, top with a third of the spinach mixture, repeat with another third of the lasagne sheets, remaining chicken mixture and a third of spinach mixture. Top with remaining lasagne sheets and spinach mixture. *[Can be made ahead to this stage. Cover; refrigerate overnight or freeze.]* Cover lasagne with foil; bake in moderate oven 40 minutes. Remove foil; bake about 30 minutes or until browned lightly.

SERVES 4

WARM TANDOORI CHICKEN SALAD

We used chilli-flavoured pappadums here, but you use any one of the different varieties of these crunchy Indian flatbreads.

6 pappadums
vegetable oil, for deep-frying
800g chicken thigh fillets, sliced thickly
1/2 cup (125ml) yogurt
2 tablespoons tandoori paste
3 teaspoons finely grated lemon rind
2 tablespoons lemon juice
2 cloves garlic, crushed
2 teaspoons ground cumin
2 (260g) Lebanese cucumbers
200g rocket leaves
1 large (350g) red capsicum, sliced thinly
1 large (300g) red onion, sliced thinly

LEMON CUMIN DRESSING
1/4 cup (60ml) peanut oil
1/4 cup (60ml) lemon juice
11/2 tablespoons mango chutney
11/2 teaspoons ground cumin

Deep-fry pappadums in hot oil until puffed and crisp; drain on absorbent paper.

Combine chicken, yogurt, paste, rind, juice, garlic and cumin in large bowl. Cover; refrigerate 3 hours or overnight. *[Can be made ahead to this stage.]*

Cook chicken on heated oiled griddle (or grill or barbecue), in batches, until browned both sides and cooked through. Cover to keep warm.

Peel thin ribbons of cucumber; combine in large bowl with rocket, capsicum and onion. Add chicken and Lemon Cumin Dressing; toss gently to combine. Just before serving, add lightly broken pappadums.

Lemon Cumin Dressing Combine all ingredients in jar; shake well.

SERVES 4

Crackle bowls and plate and bean ball from Orson & Blake Collectables

GARLIC ROASTED CHICKEN ON BRAISED WHITE BEANS

16 chicken wings
5 cloves garlic, crushed
1 tablespoon ground cumin
1/3 cup (80ml) lemon juice
1/3 cup (80ml) honey
2 tablespoons soy sauce

BRAISED WHITE BEANS
1 cup (200g) dried cannellini beans
50g butter
1 medium (170g) red onion, sliced thinly
2 bird's-eye chillies, chopped finely
2 teaspoons ground cumin
2 tablespoons lime juice
2 tablespoons Worcestershire sauce
2 teaspoons sugar
2/3 cup (160ml) chicken stock

Combine chicken, garlic, cumin, juice, honey and soy sauce in large bowl; mix well. Cover; refrigerate for several hours or overnight. *[Must be made ahead to this stage. Cover; refrigerate as directed or freeze.]*

Drain chicken over large bowl; reserve marinade. Place chicken on wire rack in baking dish; bake in hot oven, brushing occasionally with the reserved marinade, about 30 minutes or until browned and cooked through. Serve chicken with Braised White Beans.

Braised White Beans Place beans in medium bowl, cover with water; soak overnight. Rinse beans in cold water; drain. Add the beans to large pan of boiling water; simmer, uncovered, about 40 minutes or until just tender. Drain. Melt butter in same pan; cook onion, chilli and cumin, stirring, until onion is soft. Add beans and remaining ingredients; bring to boil. Simmer, uncovered, until beans are hot. *[Can be made ahead. Cover; refrigerate up to 2 days.]*

SERVES 4

Top left Spinach and chicken lasagne
Left Warm tandoori chicken salad
Above Garlic roasted chicken on braised white beans

CHICKEN CURRY WITH ONION PILAU

4 (640g) chicken thigh cutlets
4 (600g) chicken drumsticks
1/3 cup (50g) plain flour
1 1/2 tablespoons vegetable oil
2 large (400g) brown onions, sliced thickly
2 cloves garlic, crushed
1/2 teaspoon chilli powder
1 tablespoon ground cumin
1/3 cup (40g) curry powder
2 x 440g cans tomatoes
1/4 cup (60ml) tomato paste
1 tablespoon brown sugar
1 litre (4 cups) chicken stock

ONION PILAU
20g butter
2 large (400g) brown onions, chopped finely
2 teaspoons cumin seeds
1 1/2 cups (300g) basmati rice
3 cups (750ml) chicken stock

Remove skin from chicken pieces; discard skin. Toss chicken in flour, shake off excess. Heat 1 tablespoon of the oil in large pan; cook chicken, in batches, until browned. Drain on absorbent paper. Heat remaining oil in pan; cook onion, garlic, chilli, cumin and curry powder, stirring, until fragrant. Return chicken to pan with the undrained crushed tomatoes, paste, sugar and stock. Bring to boil; simmer, covered, 30 minutes. Simmer, uncovered, about 30 minutes or until chicken is tender. *[Can be made ahead to this stage. Cover; refrigerate overnight or freeze.]* Serve chicken with Onion Pilau.

Onion Pilau Heat butter in medium pan; cook onion and seeds, stirring, until onion is browned lightly. Add rice; cook, stirring, 1 minute. Stir in stock; simmer, covered, about 15 minutes or until rice is just tender. Remove from heat, fluff rice with a fork; stand, covered, 5 minutes.

SERVES 4

DRUMSTICKS WITH POTATO-SPINACH BAKE

2 teaspoons olive oil
1 small (80g) brown onion, chopped finely
1 small (130g) tomato, chopped finely
2 tablespoons tomato paste
pinch chilli flakes
2 tablespoons coarsely grated cheddar cheese
3/4 cup (50g) stale breadcrumbs
8 (1.2kg) chicken drumsticks
1 clove garlic, crushed

POTATO-SPINACH BAKE

250g spinach or silverbeet, trimmed
4 medium (800g) potatoes,
  sliced thinly
1 cup (250ml) cream
2 cloves garlic, crushed
2 tablespoons seeded mustard

Heat half the oil in small non-stick pan; cook onion, stirring, until soft. Add tomato, paste and chilli; cook, stirring, about 5 minutes or until liquid has evaporated. Stir in cheese and breadcrumbs. *[Can be made ahead to this stage. Cover; refrigerate overnight.]*

Loosen skin on drumsticks by sliding fingers between skin and meat. Gently push 1 tablespoon cooled tomato mixture under skin of each drumstick, secure with toothpicks; place on oven tray. Brush drumsticks all over with combined remaining oil and garlic.

Bake, uncovered, in moderate oven about 40 minutes or until drumsticks are browned and cooked through. Serve with Potato-Spinach Bake.

Potato-Spinach Bake Boil, steam or microwave spinach until just wilted; drain. Squeeze out excess liquid from spinach; chop finely. Layer a third of

potato over base of oiled deep 19cm square cake pan. Sprinkle with half the spinach; pour over a third of combined cream, garlic and mustard. Repeat layering, then top with remaining potato and cream mixture. Cover with foil; bake vegetable mixture in moderate oven for 1 hour. Remove foil; bake vegetable mixture about 30 minutes or until tender and browned lightly. Stand 10 minutes before serving.

SERVES 4

Left Chicken curry with onion pilau
Above Drumsticks with potato-spinach bake

CHICKEN AND CORN TURNOVERS

1 tablespoon vegetable oil
500g minced chicken
1 medium (200g) red capsicum, chopped finely
310g can creamed corn
2 green onions, chopped finely
6 sheets ready-rolled puff pastry
1 egg, beaten lightly

Heat oil in large pan; cook chicken, stirring, until browned. Add capsicum; cook, stirring, until tender. Remove from heat; stir in corn and onion, cool.

Cut four 11cm rounds from each pastry sheet. Divide chicken mixture among rounds; spread carefully, leaving a 1cm border. Brush around edges with egg; fold over to enclose filling. Press edges together to seal. Place the turnovers on oiled oven trays; brush with egg. *[Can be made ahead to this stage. Cover; refrigerate overnight or freeze.]* Bake, uncovered, in hot oven about 15 minutes or until browned.

MAKES 24

BRAISED CHICKEN AND VEGETABLES WITH RAG PASTA

1.2kg chicken
3 litres (12 cups) water
1 teaspoon black peppercorns
1 medium (150g) brown onion, chopped coarsely
4 trimmed (300g) celery sticks, chopped finely
2 tablespoons vegetable oil
2 small (200g) red onions, chopped finely
3 cloves garlic, crushed
2 medium (240g) carrots, chopped finely
1/2 cup firmly packed fresh oregano leaves
375g fresh lasagne sheets

Combine chicken, the water, peppercorns, brown onion and half the celery in large pan; bring to boil then simmer, covered, 1¹/₂ hours. Strain over large bowl; reserve chicken and stock, discard vegetables and peppercorns. Remove flesh from chicken; discard skin and bones, chop meat coarsely. *[Can be made ahead to this stage. Cover chicken and stock, separately; refrigerate overnight. Stock suitable to freeze.]*

Heat oil in large pan; cook red onion and garlic, stirring, until onion is soft. Add remaining celery, carrot and oregano; cook, stirring, until carrot is tender. Remove and discard fat from surface of cooled stock; add stock to pan, bring to boil. Tear lasagne sheets into rough pieces, add to stock with chicken; simmer, uncovered, about 5 minutes or until pasta is just tender and chicken is heated through. *[Can be made a day ahead. Cover; refrigerate overnight.]*

SERVES 6

CHICKEN OSSO BUCO

8 (1.3kg) chicken thigh cutlets
1/4 cup (35g) plain flour
2 tablespoons vegetable oil
1 large (500g) leek, sliced thickly
1 clove garlic, crushed
2 tablespoons tomato paste
2¹/₂ cups (625ml) chicken stock
1/4 cup (60ml) dry white wine
400g can tomatoes
2 trimmed (150g) celery sticks, chopped coarsely
1 medium (120g) carrot, chopped coarsely

GREMOLADA
2 tablespoons finely grated lemon rind
1/4 cup finely chopped fresh parsley
2 cloves garlic, crushed

Remove and discard skin and excess fat from chicken. Reserve 1 tablespoon of the flour; toss chicken in remaining flour, shake off excess. Heat half the oil in large pan; cook chicken, in batches, until browned. Drain on absorbent paper.

Heat remaining oil in same pan; cook leek and garlic, stirring, until leek is soft. Add the reserved flour and paste; cook, stirring, 1 minute. Stir in stock, wine and undrained chopped tomatoes; bring to boil. Return chicken to pan; simmer, covered, for 1¹/₄ hours. Add celery and carrot; simmer, uncovered, 20 minutes or until vegetables are soft. *[Can be made a day ahead. Cover; refrigerate overnight or freeze.]* Just before serving, sprinkle over Gremolada.

Gremolada Combine rind, parsley and garlic in small bowl; mix well.

SERVES 4

Top left Braised chicken and vegetables with rag pasta
Left Chicken and corn turnovers
Above Chicken osso buco

CHICKEN MACARONI BAKE

2 tablespoons vegetable oil
2 large (400g) brown onions,
  chopped finely
4 (440g) chicken thigh fillets,
  sliced thinly
2 teaspoons chicken stock powder
1 cup (250ml) dry white wine
300ml thickened cream
1 cup finely chopped fresh
  basil leaves
250g macaroni
6 medium (1.2kg) potatoes,
  chopped coarsely
2 cloves garlic, crushed
1/4 cup (60ml) sour cream
1.2kg pumpkin, chopped coarsely
1/2 cup (35g) stale breadcrumbs

Heat oil in large pan; cook onion, stirring, until soft. Add chicken; cook, stirring, about 5 minutes or until browned and almost cooked through. Stir in combined stock powder and wine; bring to boil. Simmer, uncovered, about 5 minutes or until wine is reduced by half. Stir in cream; simmer, uncovered, for about 10 minutes or until mixture thickens. Stir in basil.

Meanwhile, cook pasta in large pan of boiling water, uncovered, until just tender; drain. Combine pasta with chicken mixture.

Boil, steam or microwave potato and pumpkin, separately, until tender; drain. Mash potato in large bowl with garlic and sour cream until smooth; spread potato mixture over base of oiled shallow 2.5 litre (12-cup capacity) ovenproof dish. Top with half the chicken mixture. Mash pumpkin in same large bowl until smooth; carefully spread pumpkin over chicken layer. Top with remaining chicken mixture. *[Can be made ahead to this stage. Cover; refrigerate overnight.]* Sprinkle top with the breadcrumbs; bake, uncovered, in moderate oven about 35 minutes or until browned lightly.

SERVES 4 TO 6

APRICOT CHICKEN WITH CREAMY RICE

12 (1.8kg) chicken drumsticks
2 tablespoons vegetable oil
2 large (400g) brown onions,
  sliced thickly
2 teaspoons grated fresh ginger
2 cloves garlic, crushed
425g can apricot nectar
1 cup (250ml) water
40g packet French onion soup mix
1 cup (200g) calrose rice
1 tablespoon finely chopped
  fresh parsley

Remove and discard skin from chicken. Heat half the oil in large pan; cook chicken, in batches, until browned all over. Drain on absorbent paper. Heat remaining oil in same pan; cook onion, ginger and garlic, stirring, for about 5 minutes or until onion is browned lightly. Return chicken to pan with nectar, the water and dry soup mix; bring to boil. Simmer, covered, 10 minutes. Add the rice; simmer, uncovered, stirring occasionally, about 30 minutes or until rice is tender. Just before serving, gently stir in parsley.

SERVES 4

Left Chicken macaroni bake
Top right Apricot chicken with creamy rice
Right Bonza-burgers

Square plate from Orson & Blake Collectables

BONZA-BURGERS

500g minced chicken
1 medium (120g) zucchini,
grated coarsely
1 medium (120g) carrot,
grated coarsely
2 tablespoons plain flour
2 teaspoons Cajun Seasoning
4 wholemeal bread rolls
2 medium (380g) tomatoes, seeded,
chopped finely
1 tablespoon finely chopped
fresh chives
2 teaspoons olive oil
4 large lettuce leaves
1/3 cup (80ml) sour cream
1/4 teaspoon hot paprika

Using hand, combine chicken, zucchini, carrot, flour and Seasoning in large bowl; shape mixture into 4 patties. *[Can be made ahead to this stage. Cover; refrigerate overnight or freeze.]* Cook patties in large heated oiled pan until browned both sides and cooked through.

Meanwhile, split rolls in half; toast cut sides until browned lightly. Combine tomato, chives and oil in small bowl. To serve, sandwich burgers, lettuce, tomato mixture and combined sour cream and paprika between roll halves.

SERVES 4

CHILLI CHICKEN NOODLE STIR-FRY

Tat soi is an Asian green vegetable. It can be replaced with Chinese broccoli or spinach leaves, if you prefer.

- 4 (440g) chicken thigh fillets, sliced thinly
- 2 tablespoons finely chopped fresh coriander leaves
- 2 cloves garlic, crushed
- 4 bird's-eye chillies, chopped finely
- 2 x 85g packets instant noodles
- 2 tablespoons vegetable oil
- 1 medium (150g) brown onion, sliced thinly
- 1 large (350g) red capsicum, sliced thinly

Spiral bowls from Made in Japan

GRANDMOTHER'S CHICKEN

- 2 tablespoons vegetable oil
- 1 large (200g) brown onion, sliced thickly
- 2 cloves garlic, crushed
- 4 (640g) chicken thigh cutlets
- 4 (600g) chicken drumsticks
- 4 sprigs fresh rosemary
- 4 medium (800g) potatoes, chopped coarsely
- 2 medium (380g) tomatoes, chopped coarsely
- 1/2 cup (125ml) chicken stock

- 150g button mushrooms, halved
- 4 bacon rashers, chopped coarsely
- 1/2 cup (80g) seeded black olives

Heat oil in large flameproof baking dish; cook onion and garlic, stirring, until onion is soft. Add chicken; cook, stirring, until just browned all over. Add rosemary, potato, tomato and stock. Bake chicken mixture, uncovered, in hot oven 1 hour. Stir in mushrooms, bacon and olives; bake, uncovered, about 20 minutes or until potato is crisp and chicken tender.

SERVES 4

350g baby bok choy,
   chopped coarsely
100g baby tat soi
2 green onions, sliced thinly
2 tablespoons oyster sauce

Combine chicken, coriander, garlic and chilli in large bowl; mix well. Cover; refrigerate 2 hours or overnight. *[Can be made ahead to this stage and frozen.]*

Discard flavour sachets from noodles; cook noodles according to instructions on packet, drain.

Heat half the oil in wok; stir-fry chicken, in batches, until browned and cooked through. Heat remaining oil in wok; stir-fry brown onion and capsicum 2 minutes. Return chicken to wok with noodles; stir-fry 2 minutes. Add bok choy, tat soi, green onion and oyster sauce; stir-fry until leaves are just wilted.

SERVES 4

CHICKEN, KUMARA AND POTATO CUSTARD

1.2kg chicken
2.5 litres (10 cups) water
**1 trimmed (75g) celery stick,
   chopped coarsely**
**2 large (400g) brown onions,
   chopped coarsely**
**4 medium (800g) potatoes,
   chopped coarsely**
**2 medium (800g) kumara,
   chopped coarsely**
1 tablespoon olive oil
3 cloves garlic, crushed
**1 cup (125g) coarsely grated
   cheddar cheese**
2 cups (500ml) cream
5 eggs, beaten lightly

Combine chicken, the water, celery and half of the onion in large pan; bring to boil. Simmer, uncovered, about 1½ hours or until chicken is tender. Strain over large bowl; reserve stock for another purpose.

Remove flesh from chicken; discard skin and bones, chop meat coarsely.

Meanwhile, boil, steam or microwave potato and kumara until just tender, drain; mash together in large bowl. *[Can be prepared ahead to this stage. Cover, chicken and mashed mixture, separately; refrigerate overnight.]*

Heat oil in small pan; cook remaining onion and garlic, stirring, until onion is soft. Combine onion mixture, chicken and remaining ingredients with mashed mixture; mix well. Spread in oiled shallow 2.75-litre (11-cup capacity) ovenproof dish. Bake custard, uncovered, in moderate oven about 1¼ hours or until browned and set.

SERVES 4

Far left Grandmother's chicken
Left Chilli chicken noodle stir-fry
Above Chicken, kumara and potato custard

Dinner bells ring for sea-fare

Abundant and healthful, seafood should be a regular fixture at our table but it's too often believed that fish is more expensive than other meats. Here, enjoy the fruits of the sea without breaking the bank

MUSSELS WITH CORIANDER AND BROAD BEANS

1kg mussels
90g butter
2 medium (300g) brown onions,
  chopped finely
3 cloves garlic, crushed
1/2 cup (125ml) dry white wine
1/2 cup (125ml) lemon juice
1/2 cup (125ml) water
500g packet frozen broad beans,
  cooked, peeled
1/3 cup finely chopped fresh
  coriander leaves
1/4 cup finely chopped fresh parsley

Scrub mussels, remove beards. *[Can be prepared ahead to this stage. Cover; refrigerate overnight.]*

Heat butter in large pan; cook onion and garlic, stirring, until onion is soft. Add wine; simmer, uncovered, until reduced by half. Add juice and water; bring to boil. Add mussels; simmer, covered, about 2 minutes or until mussels open. Discard any unopened mussels, add beans and herbs; simmer for 2 minutes.

SERVES 4

TUNA, BEAN AND GRILLED VEGETABLE SALAD

1 medium (200g) red capsicum
1 medium (200g) yellow capsicum
1 large (200g) brown onion
4 large (600g) zucchini
1/3 cup olive oil
200g button mushrooms, halved
400g can cannellini beans,
  drained, rinsed
425g can tuna, drained, flaked
1/4 cup (60ml) lemon juice
1 clove garlic, crushed
1 tablespoon finely chopped
  fresh parsley

Quarter capsicums, remove and discard seeds and membranes. Roast under grill or in very hot oven, skin-side up, until skin blisters and blackens. Cover capsicum pieces in plastic or paper for 5 minutes, peel away skin; cut capsicum into thick strips.

Cut onion into 8 wedges; cut zucchini diagonally into 1cm slices. Place onion and zucchini on oven tray; brush with 1 tablespoon of the oil. Grill onion and zucchini until browned lightly both sides.

Heat 1 tablespoon of the oil in small pan; cook mushrooms, stirring, until browned lightly.

Combine capsicum, onion, zucchini, mushrooms, beans and tuna in large bowl; gently toss with combined remaining oil, juice, garlic and parsley.

SERVES 4

From left Mussels with coriander and broad beans; Tuna, bean and grilled vegetable salad

CRUMBED SMOKED HADDOCK FLORENTINE

600g smoked haddock
400g spinach, trimmed
1 cup (125g) coarsely grated
cheddar cheese
1/3 cup finely chopped fresh chives
2/3 cup (160ml) cream
1 cup (70g) stale breadcrumbs
40g butter

Place fish in large pan; cover with cold water, bring to boil, drain. Repeat process; chop fish coarsely. Boil, steam or microwave spinach until just wilted; drain. Squeeze excess liquid from spinach; chop coarsely. *[Can be made ahead to this stage. Cover, separately; refrigerate overnight.]*

Place half the fish in oiled 1.25-litre (5-cup capacity) ovenproof dish; top with half the spinach, a third of the cheese, half the chives and half the cream. Repeat layering, finishing with remaining cream. Sprinkle with combined breadcrumbs and remaining cheese; drizzle with melted butter. Bake, uncovered, in hot oven about 40 minutes or until browned.

SERVES 4

Teatowel from Accoutrement

KEDGEREE

You will need approximately 1¹/₄ cups of uncooked long-grain rice for this recipe.

1 tablespoon vegetable oil
1 medium (150g) brown onion, chopped finely
1 tablespoon mild curry paste
3 cups cooked long-grain white rice
415g can salmon, drained, flaked
1/4 cup (60ml) cream
2 hard-boiled eggs
2 tablespoons finely chopped fresh parsley

Heat oil in large pan; cook onion, stirring, until soft. Add curry paste; cook, stirring, until fragrant. Stir in rice, salmon and cream; cook, stirring, until hot. Just before serving, cut each egg into 6 wedges and gently stir through Kedgeree; sprinkle with parsley.

SERVES 4

Plate and fork from Empire; bowls and basket from Shack Homewares

FETTUCCINE WITH OCTOPUS IN TOMATO SAUCE

2 cloves garlic, unpeeled
1/4 cup (60ml) olive oil
4 large (1kg) tomatoes, quartered
2 medium (300g) brown onions,
  chopped finely
1/4 cup (60ml) dry white wine
2 bird's-eye chillies, chopped finely
2 tablespoons tomato paste
1kg baby octopus
375g fettuccine

Brush garlic cloves with a little of the oil; wrap in foil. Place garlic in shallow baking dish. Add tomato; drizzle with 1 tablespoon of the oil. Bake tomato and garlic, uncovered, in moderate oven about 20 minutes or until the tomato is tender. Remove garlic from foil; discard skin, chop garlic finely.

Heat 1 tablespoon of the remaining oil in medium pan; cook onion, stirring, until soft. Add wine; cook, stirring, until wine is reduced by half. Add tomato, garlic, chilli and paste; cook, stirring, until hot. *[Can be made ahead to this stage. Cover; refrigerate up to 2 days or freeze.]*

Remove and discard heads and beaks from octopus; cut each octopus into quarters. Combine with remaining oil in large bowl; mix well. Cook octopus, in batches, in large heated non-stick pan until browned and tender.

Meanwhile, cook pasta in large pan of boiling water, uncovered, until just tender; drain. Just before serving, gently toss tomato mixture and octopus in large bowl with pasta.

SERVES 4 TO 6

Placemat, plate and napkin from Orson & Blake Collectables

Top left Kedgeree
Left Fettuccine with octopus in tomato sauce
Right Crumbed smoked haddock florentine

ANCHOVY SUPPLI

2 cups (400g) calrose rice
2 teaspoons olive oil
2 x 45g cans anchovy fillets in oil,
    drained, chopped finely
2 cloves garlic, crushed
2 tablespoons tomato paste
1 tablespoon finely chopped
    fresh parsley
2 tablespoons finely grated
    parmesan cheese
125g mozzarella cheese
plain flour
2 eggs, beaten lightly
1 cup (100g) packaged breadcrumbs
vegetable oil, for deep-frying

TOMATO SAUCE

1 trimmed (75g) celery stick,
    chopped finely
1 small (80g) brown onion,
    chopped finely
1 clove garlic, crushed
1/2 cup (125ml) tomato paste
1 1/2 cups (375ml) water

Cook rice in large pan of boiling water, uncovered, until just tender; drain.

Heat oil in small pan; cook anchovy, garlic, paste and parsley until fragrant. Combine rice and anchovy mixture in large bowl with parmesan; mix well.

Cut mozzarella into 1cm cubes. Flatten 1 level tablespoon cooled rice mixture in one hand, top with a cube of mozzarella, then cover mozzarella with another level tablespoon rice mixture. Carefully shape rice mixture for suppli into balls. Coat suppli in flour; dip in egg then breadcrumbs. [Can be made a day ahead to this stage. Cover; refrigerate overnight.]

Heat oil in large pan; deep-fry suppli, in batches, until golden brown. Drain on absorbent paper. Serve suppli with Tomato Sauce.

Tomato Sauce Cook celery, onion and garlic in small heated non-stick pan, stirring, until celery is soft. Stir in paste and the water, bring to boil; simmer, uncovered, about 15 minutes or until sauce thickens. [Can be made a day ahead. Cover; refrigerate overnight.]

SERVES 6 TO 8

CHILLI FISH WITH ROAST TOMATO SAUCE AND LENTILS

800g redfish fillets
6 bird's-eye chillies, seeded,
    chopped finely
3 cloves garlic, crushed
1 teaspoon salt
4 large (1kg) tomatoes, halved
1 tablespoon finely chopped fresh
    lemon thyme
2 tablespoons vegetable oil
2 teaspoons coriander seeds
1 cup (200g) brown lentils, rinsed
3 cups (750ml) chicken stock
2 cloves garlic, crushed, extra
40g butter
1 tablespoon vegetable oil, extra

Place fish in large bowl with combined chilli, garlic and salt; mix well. Cover; refrigerate 3 hours or overnight.

Combine tomato, thyme, oil and seeds in medium baking dish; bake, uncovered, in very hot oven about 40 minutes or until tomato is soft. Blend or process tomato mixture until coarsely pureed; cover to keep warm.

Combine lentils, stock and extra garlic in medium pan, bring to boil; simmer, uncovered, about 15 minutes or until lentils are just tender. [Can be made ahead to this stage. Cover tomato mixture and lentil mixture, separately; refrigerate overnight.]

Heat butter and extra oil in large pan; cook fish, in batches, until browned both sides and cooked as desired. Place fish on individual serving plates with portions of roasted tomato sauce and lentils.

SERVES 8

Left Anchovy suppli
Right Chilli fish with roast tomato sauce and lentils

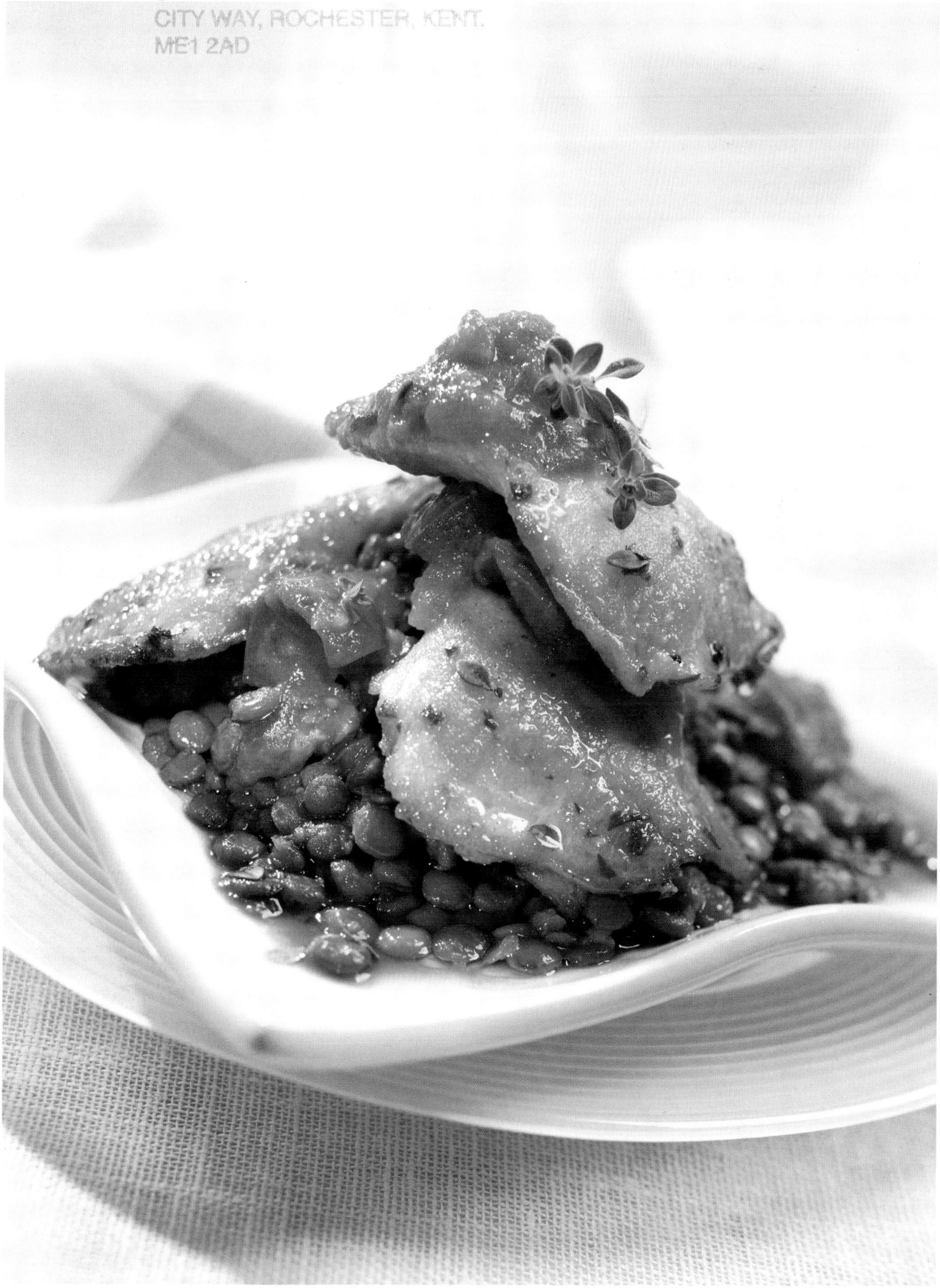

Large bowl from Shack Homewares; placemat from Empire; fabric from Ruby Star Traders

MUSSELS WITH TOMATOES AND WHITE WINE

1 cup (200g) long-grain white rice
1kg small black mussels
1 tablespoon olive oil
1 medium (150g) brown onion, chopped finely
2 cloves garlic, crushed
1/3 cup (80ml) dry white wine
400g can tomatoes
1/2 cup (125ml) water
1/2 teaspoon sugar
1 tablespoon finely chopped fresh parsley

Cook rice in large pan of boiling water, uncovered, until just tender; drain. Cover rice to keep warm.

Scrub mussels, remove beards. Heat oil in large pan; cook onion and garlic, stirring, until onion is soft. Add wine, undrained crushed tomatoes, the water and sugar; simmer, uncovered, for about 5 minutes or until sauce thickens. Add mussels; simmer, covered, for about 3 minutes or until mussels open. Discard any unopened mussels. Just before serving, sprinkle parsley over mussels; serve with rice.

SERVES 4

Fork and plate from Empire; cloth from Ruby Star Traders

SALMON AND DILL FRITTATA

2 medium (400g) potatoes, halved
1 tablespoon olive oil
2 medium (300g) brown onions,
    sliced thinly
8 eggs, beaten lightly
1/2 cup (125ml) cream
1 teaspoon dried dill
415g can pink salmon,
    drained, flaked
3/4 cup (180ml) sour cream
1 tablespoon lemon juice
1 teaspoon cracked black pepper

Oil deep 22cm round cake pan; line base with baking paper.

Boil, steam or microwave potato until just tender; drain, slice thinly. Heat oil in medium pan; cook onion, stirring, until soft. Combine eggs, cream and dill in large bowl. Place a third of the potato over base of prepared pan. Sprinkle over half of both the salmon and the onion; repeat layering, finishing with potato. Pour egg mixture over the top; bake, uncovered, in moderately slow oven about 50 minutes or until set. Serve frittata with combined sour cream, juice and pepper.

TUNA PASTA BAKE

Canned salmon can be used in place of the tuna in this recipe.

200g shell pasta
4 sprigs fresh parsley
1/2 small (40g) brown onion,
    chopped coarsely
2 bay leaves
6 black peppercorns
3 cups (750ml) milk
60g butter
2 tablespoons plain flour
2 tablespoons dry white wine
1 tablespoon seeded mustard
425g can tuna, drained
1 cup (125g) coarsely grated
    cheddar cheese
1 cup (70g) stale breadcrumbs

Cook pasta in large pan of boiling water, uncovered, until just tender; drain.

Combine parsley, onion, leaves, peppercorns and milk in medium pan; bring to boil. Remove from heat; cover, stand 5 minutes. Strain into medium bowl; discard vegetables and spices.

Heat butter in large pan. Add flour; cook, stirring, until mixture thickens and bubbles. Gradually stir in the infused milk; stir until sauce boils and thickens. Stir wine and mustard into sauce. Combine pasta and tuna with sauce; mix well. Place mixture in oiled deep 2-litre (8-cup capacity) ovenproof dish; sprinkle with combined cheese and breadcrumbs. *[Can be made ahead to this stage. Cover; refrigerate overnight.]* Bake, uncovered, in moderate oven about 25 minutes or until heated through and browned lightly.

SERVES 4

Top left Mussels with tomatoes and white wine
Left Tuna pasta bake
Above Salmon and dill frittata

Use any firm white fish fillets you desire. You need to soak 12 bamboo skewers in water at least 1 hour before using to avoid scorching.

600g white fish fillets
1/3 cup (80ml) soy sauce
1/4 cup (60ml) peanut oil
1 tablespoon sambal oelek
2 tablespoons lemon juice
3/4 cup finely chopped fresh coriander leaves
1 large (200g) brown onion

GRAPEFRUIT-SCENTED FISH AND POTATO SLICE

4 medium (800g) potatoes, quartered
2 tablespoons vegetable oil
3 medium (450g) onions, sliced thinly
3 cloves garlic, crushed
1 tablespoon sugar
3 medium (570g) tomatoes, sliced thickly
1/3 cup firmly packed fresh oregano leaves
1 cup (125g) grated cheddar cheese
500g white fish fillets
1/2 cup (125ml) grapefruit juice
1/2 cup (125ml) cream

BUTTERED BEANS

500g green beans, halved
60g butter
1 tablespoon finely grated grapefruit rind

Boil, steam or microwave potatoes until just tender; drain, slice thinly. Heat oil in medium pan; cook onion, garlic and sugar, stirring, until onion is soft.

Layer half the potato over base of oiled deep 19cm square cake pan. Top with half the onion mixture, half the tomato, half the oregano, half the cheese and all the fish. Repeat with remaining potato, onion mixture, tomato, oregano and cheese. Pour combined juice and cream over the top; bake, uncovered, in moderate oven about 50 minutes or until browned lightly and cooked through. Stand 10 minutes; pour off excess pan juices. Serve slice with Buttered Beans.

Buttered Beans Boil, steam or microwave beans until just tender; drain. Melt butter in medium pan, add beans and rind; cook, stirring, until hot.

SERVES 4

2 medium (400g) green capsicums
2 medium (240g) green zucchini
250g rice vermicelli
6 green onions, sliced thinly
½ cup (125ml) chicken stock

Remove and discard any skin and bones from fish; cut fish into 3cm pieces.

Combine sauce, 2 tablespoons of the oil, sambal, juice and coriander in large bowl; reserve two-thirds of soy mixture. Place fish in bowl with remaining one-third soy mixture; mix well. Cover marinated fish and remaining soy mixture, separately; refrigerate 3 hours or overnight. *[Best made ahead to this stage.]*

Cut brown onion into thick wedges, cut 1 capsicum into 2cm pieces, slice zucchini thickly. Thread vegetable pieces onto 6 of the skewers. Place vermicelli in medium heatproof bowl, cover with boiling water, stand only until just tender; drain. Slice remaining capsicum into thin strips. Thread fish onto remaining 6 skewers.

Cook fish and vegetable kebabs, in batches, on heated oiled griddle (or grill or barbecue) until vegetables are browned and tender and fish is cooked through.

Meanwhile, heat remaining oil in wok or large pan; stir-fry green onion and capsicum strips until soft. Add vermicelli,

stock and half of the reserved soy mixture; stir-fry until hot.

Serve kebabs with fried vermicelli, drizzled with remaining soy mixture.

SERVES 4

Left Grapefruit-scented fish and vegetable slice
Below Pac-rim fish and vegetable kebabs

Almost vegetarian

No stodgy "nuts-and-berries" food here... just a delightful selection of the most delicious and innovative recipes using rice, grains and greens you could ever imagine – and not one dependent on meat for its flavour

POTATO, SILVERBEET AND TOFU CURRY

1 tablespoon vegetable oil
2 medium (300g) brown onions, chopped finely
2 cloves garlic, crushed
1 tablespoon finely grated fresh ginger
1 teaspoon ground nutmeg
2 teaspoons ground cumin
1 teaspoon cayenne pepper
1 teaspoon ground turmeric
1 teaspoon garam masala
1/4 cup finely chopped fresh coriander leaves
1 litre (4 cups) vegetable stock
6 medium (1.2kg) potatoes, chopped
250g firm tofu
2 tablespoons plain flour
1 egg, beaten lightly
2 tablespoons sesame seeds
vegetable oil, for shallow-frying
1kg silverbeet, trimmed

Heat the 1 tablespoon of oil in large pan; cook onion, stirring, until soft. Add garlic, ginger and spices; cook, stirring, until fragrant. Stir in coriander, stock and potato; simmer, covered, about 30 minutes or until potato is just soft. *[Can be made ahead to this stage. Cover, refrigerate overnight or freeze.]*
Meanwhile, cut tofu into 2cm cubes; toss in flour, shake off excess. Dip tofu in egg; toss in sesame seeds. Heat vegetable oil, shallow-fry tofu until browned lightly; drain on absorbent paper.
Just before serving, add coarsely chopped silverbeet to potato mixture; simmer, stirring, until silverbeet is just wilted. Top with tofu.

SERVES 4

VEGETARIAN TAGINE

1 tablespoon olive oil
1 medium (150g) brown onion, chopped coarsely
1 clove garlic, crushed
1 1/2 tablespoons ground cumin
1 tablespoon ground coriander
2 teaspoons caraway seeds
2 medium (600g) eggplants, chopped
1 large (150g) zucchini, chopped
4 medium (760g) tomatoes, chopped
300g can chickpeas, drained, rinsed
1 tablespoon lemon juice
1 cup (250ml) vegetable stock
1/3 cup chopped fresh coriander leaves

Heat oil in large pan; cook onion, garlic, spices, seeds and eggplant, stirring, until onion is soft. Add zucchini, tomato and chickpeas; cook, stirring, about 5 minutes or until vegetables are just tender. Stir in juice and stock; cook, uncovered, until mixture boils and thickens. *[Can be made a day ahead. Cover; refrigerate overnight or freeze.]* Just before serving, stir in coriander. Serve Vegetarian Tagine with couscous, if desired.

SERVES 4

From top Potato, silverbeet and tofu curry; Vegetarian tagine

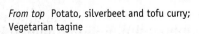

SWEET CHILLI VEGETABLE, NOODLE AND TOFU STIR-FRY

We used a 5mm-wide rice stick noodle (called sen lek on the package) in this recipe.

300g firm tofu
375g rice noodles
1/4 cup (60ml) peanut oil
2 medium (300g) brown onions, sliced thinly
2 cloves garlic, crushed
200g button mushrooms, sliced thinly
300g baby bok choy, chopped coarsely
1 tablespoon white vinegar
1/2 cup (125ml) sweet chilli sauce
100g tat soi

Cut tofu into 2cm cubes; drain tofu on absorbent paper.

Place noodles in large heatproof bowl, cover with boiling water; stand until just tender. Drain; cover to keep warm.

Heat 2 tablespoons of the oil in wok or large pan; stir-fry tofu, in batches, until browned lightly. Drain on absorbent paper. Heat remaining oil in same pan; stir-fry onion and garlic until onion is soft. Add mushrooms; stir-fry until mushrooms are tender. Add bok choy, noodles and vinegar and sauce; stir-fry until hot. Add tat soi; stir-fry until tat soi is barely wilted. Toss tofu gently through mixture; serve immediately.

SERVES 4

LEEK AND PUMPKIN FILLO PARCELS

800g pumpkin, chopped
30g butter
2 medium (700g) leeks, chopped coarsely
3/4 cup (90g) coarsely grated cheddar cheese
2 tablespoons seeded mustard
375g packet fillo pastry
2/3 cup (160ml) vegetable oil

Boil, steam or microwave pumpkin until just tender; drain. Meanwhile, heat the butter in medium pan; cook leek, stirring, until soft. Combine pumpkin and leek in large bowl with cheese and mustard; mix well. *[Can be made ahead to this stage. Cover; refrigerate overnight.]*

Cover fillo pastry with damp tea-towel to prevent drying out. Working with 3 fillo sheets at a time, brush each sheet lightly with oil; fold in half. Place 1/2 cup of vegetable mixture at one end of folded fillo; roll to enclose filling, folding in sides of fillo as you roll. Repeat with remaining vegetable mixture and fillo.

Place fillo parcels on oiled oven tray; brush lightly with oil. Bake, uncovered, in moderately hot oven about 20 minutes or until pastry is browned lightly.

MAKES 8

SPINACH, CAPSICUM AND FETTA PIE

2 medium (400g) red capsicums
2kg spinach or silverbeet, trimmed
250g fetta cheese, crumbled
6 green onions, chopped coarsely
2 tablespoons finely chopped fresh mint leaves
2 tablespoons finely chopped fresh parsley
4 eggs, beaten lightly
1/4 teaspoon ground nutmeg
6 sheets fillo pastry
1/4 cup (60ml) olive oil

Quarter capsicums, remove and discard seeds and membranes. Roast under grill or in very hot oven, skin-side up, until skin blisters and blackens. Cover capsicum pieces in plastic or paper for 5 minutes, peel away skin; slice into thin strips.

Meanwhile, boil, steam or microwave coarsely chopped spinach until just wilted; drain. Squeeze excess liquid from spinach; drain on absorbent paper.

Combine spinach, capsicum, cheese, onion, mint, parsley, egg and nutmeg in large bowl; mix well. Spoon mixture into lightly oiled 22cm round pie dish.

Cover fillo pastry with damp tea-towel to prevent drying out. Brush 1 sheet of pastry with oil, fold in half lengthways; place over filling. Repeat with remaining pastry and oil, overlapping each sheet of pastry around dish. Fold and tuck in overhanging pastry; brush top with oil. Bake, uncovered, in moderately hot oven about 45 minutes or until filling is set and pastry is browned lightly.

SERVES 4

Left Sweet chilli vegetable, noodle and tofu stir-fry
Top right Leek and pumpkin fillo parcels
Right Spinach, capsicum and fetta pie

ROAST GARLIC AND POTATO PIZZA

5 medium (1kg) potatoes, halved
4 cloves garlic, crushed
1/4 cup fresh oregano leaves
1 large (200g) onion, sliced thickly
1/4 cup (60ml) olive oil
7 small (910g) tomatoes, halved
2 teaspoons sugar
**11/2 cups (150g) coarsely grated
   mozzarella cheese**
**1/4 cup finely shredded fresh
   basil leaves**

PIZZA BASE

1 teaspoon (3g) dried yeast
1/2 teaspoon sugar
2/3 cup (160ml) warm water
11/2 cups (225g) plain flour
1/2 teaspoon salt
1/4 cup (60ml) olive oil

Boil, steam or microwave potato halves until just tender; drain. Cut each potato half in half again; place in large shallow baking dish with garlic, oregano and onion, drizzle with 2 tablespoons of the oil. Bake, uncovered, in very hot oven about 20 minutes or until onion is soft and potato is browned lightly.

Meanwhile, combine tomato and remaining oil in medium baking dish; bake, uncovered, in very hot oven about 30 minutes or until tomato is browned and soft. Blend or process tomato with sugar until just roughly chopped. *[Can be made ahead to this stage. Cover, potato mixture and tomato mixture, separately; refrigerate overnight.]*

Spread tomato mixture on Pizza Base; top with 1 cup of the cheese, then the potato mixture. Sprinkle remaining cheese and basil over the top; bake in hot oven, uncovered, about 30 minutes or until cheese is browned and Pizza Base is crisp.

Pizza Base Combine yeast, sugar and 1/4 cup of the water in small bowl; cover, stand in warm place about 20 minutes or until mixture is frothy.

Place flour and salt in medium bowl. Stir in remaining water, yeast mixture and oil; mix to a soft dough. Knead dough on floured surface about 5 minutes or until smooth and elastic. Place dough in medium oiled bowl; cover, stand in warm place about 1 hour or until dough is doubled in size. Turn dough onto floured surface, knead until smooth. Roll dough to a 36cm round; place Pizza Base on oiled oven tray or pizza pan.

SERVES 4

Above Roast garlic and potato pizza
Top right Mushroom and spinach risotto
Right Roasted root vegetables with barley

MUSHROOM AND SPINACH RISOTTO

1.5 litres (6 cups) vegetable stock
1 cup (250ml) dry white wine
1/4 cup (60ml) olive oil
500g button mushrooms, sliced
**1 large (200g) brown onion,
  chopped finely**
2 cloves garlic, crushed
2 cups (400g) calrose rice
1/2 cup (125ml) sour cream
250g baby spinach leaves

Bring stock and wine to boil in large pan; cover, keep hot. Heat 2 tablespoons of the oil in large pan; cook mushrooms, stirring, until browned lightly, remove from pan. Heat remaining oil in same pan; cook onion and garlic, stirring, until onion is soft. Add rice, stir to coat in oil mixture. Stir in 1 cup of the stock mixture; cook, stirring, over low heat until liquid is absorbed. Continue adding stock mixture, in 1-cup batches, stirring, until absorbed after each addition. Total cooking time should be about 35 minutes or until rice is just tender. Remove pan from heat, stir in sour cream, spinach and mushrooms. *[Best made just before serving.]*

SERVES 4

ROASTED ROOT VEGETABLES WITH BARLEY

1 tablespoon olive oil
1 large (200g) brown onion, sliced
2 cloves garlic, crushed
**3 medium (360g) carrots,
  chopped coarsely**
**3 medium (375g) parsnips,
  chopped coarsely**
**4 medium (500g) turnips,
  chopped coarsely**
1/3 cup (80ml) honey
2 tablespoons Dijon mustard
1/3 cup (80ml) lemon juice
1.5 litres (6 cups) vegetable stock
1 1/2 cups (300g) barley
1 tablespoon chopped fresh parsley

Heat oil in large flameproof baking dish; cook onion and garlic, stirring, until onion is soft. Add carrot, parsnip and turnip; cook, stirring, 1 minute. Pour combined honey, mustard and juice over vegetables; bake, uncovered, in moderately hot oven about 1 1/4 hours or until the vegetables are browned and tender.

Meanwhile, bring stock to boil in large pan; add barley. Simmer, covered, about 25 minutes or until barley is tender and liquid is absorbed. Just before serving, stir in parsley; serve topped with vegetables.

SERVES 4

GIANT DENVER OMELETTES

This recipe makes 2 large layered omelettes.

10 eggs, beaten lightly
1 tablespoon seeded mustard

DENVER FILLING
2 teaspoons vegetable oil
1 large (200g) brown onion,
  sliced thinly
1 medium (200g) red capsicum,
  sliced thinly
100g ham, sliced thinly
1/4 cup finely chopped fresh parsley
2 small (260g) tomatoes, seeded,
  sliced thinly
1/2 cup (60g) grated cheddar cheese

Combine eggs and mustard in large jug.

Heat 23cm non-stick pan; spray with cooking oil spray. Pour 1/4 cup of the egg mixture into pan; cook, tilting pan, over medium heat until almost set. Sprinkle 1/3 cup Denver Filling over half the omelette; using a spatula, fold omelette over, in half, to enclose filling.

Pour another 1/4 cup of egg mixture into empty half of pan; mixture will spread under the first folded omelette. Cook over high heat until almost set.

Sprinkle omelette with another 1/3 cup of Denver Filling, fold omelette over, onto the top of the first folded omelette. Repeat this process 2 more times to complete one giant layered omelette. Carefully slide omelette onto plate; keep warm.

Repeat layering process to make second giant omelette using remaining egg mixture and filling. Cut omelettes in half and serve with toast, if desired.

Denver Filling Heat oil in medium pan; cook onion and capsicum, stirring, until onion is soft. Combine onion mixture with remaining ingredients in medium bowl.

SERVES 4

SOY BEANS AND RICE

1¹/₄ cups (250g) dried soy beans
1 tablespoon olive oil
2 cloves garlic, crushed
2 large (400g) brown onions, chopped finely
2 tablespoons grated lemon rind
1¹/₄ cups (250g) long-grain white rice, rinsed, drained
2¹/₂ cups (625ml) chicken stock
50g butter
1 teaspoon ground cinnamon
1¹/₃ cups (200g) dried apricots
1¹/₄ cups (210g) seeded prunes, halved
¹/₃ cup (80ml) lemon juice

Place beans in large bowl, cover with cold water; soak overnight.

Rinse and drain beans, add beans to large pan of boiling water; simmer, un-covered, about 1 hour or until beans are tender. Drain.

Heat oil in same pan; cook garlic, onion and rind, stirring, until onion is soft. Add beans, rice and stock, bring to boil; simmer, covered, about 20 minutes or until rice is just tender. [Can be made ahead to this stage. Cover; refrigerate overnight.]

Meanwhile, melt butter in medium pan; cook cinnamon, apricots, prunes and juice, stirring, until apricots are browned lightly. Serve beans and rice topped with dried fruit, drizzled with pan juices.

SERVES 4

Left Giant Denver omelettes
Above Soy beans and rice

BAKED PENNE WITH PEAS, MUSHROOMS AND LEEK

Any short pasta can be substituted for penne in this recipe.

400g penne
2 tablespoons vegetable oil
50g butter
1 clove garlic, crushed
2 small (400g) leeks, sliced
300g button mushrooms, sliced
1/3 cup finely chopped fresh chives
2 cups (250g) frozen peas, thawed

BECHAMEL SAUCE

100g butter
2/3 cup (100g) plain flour
1.25 litres (5 cups) hot milk
2 1/2 cups (310g) coarsely grated
   cheddar cheese

Cook pasta in large pan of boiling water, uncovered, until just tender; drain.

Heat oil and butter in same pan; cook garlic, leek and mushrooms, stirring, until leek softens. Combine pasta and leek mixture in large bowl with chives, peas and Bechamel Sauce. Spoon the mixture into 3.75-litre (15-cup capacity) ovenproof dish; spread with reserved 2/3 cup Bechamel Sauce. *[Can be prepared ahead to this stage. Cover; refrigerate overnight or freeze.]* Bake, uncovered, in moderate oven about 40 minutes or until browned lightly.

Bechamel Sauce Melt butter in medium pan. Add flour; cook, stirring, until mixture thickens and bubbles. Gradually stir in milk; stir until sauce boils and thickens. Remove from heat; stir in cheese. Reserve 2/3 cup of sauce for top.

SERVES 4 TO 6

KUMARA AND ZUCCHINI RISOTTO

1 large (500g) kumara, peeled,
   chopped coarsely
4 large (600g) zucchini,
   chopped coarsely
1/4 cup (60ml) olive oil
1 large (200g) brown onion,
   chopped finely
2 cloves garlic, crushed
1/2 cup (125ml) dry white wine
2 cups (400g) calrose rice
1.5 litres (6 cups) vegetable stock
2 tablespoons finely grated
   parmesan cheese
1/4 cup (60ml) cream
1 tablespoon finely chopped fresh
   basil leaves

Combine the kumara and zucchini with 2 tablespoons of the oil in large baking dish; bake, uncovered, in moderate oven 15 minutes or until kumara is browned and just tender.

Heat remaining oil in large pan; cook onion and garlic, stirring, until onion is soft. Add wine; cook, stirring, until wine is reduced by half. Add rice and stock. Bring to boil; simmer, uncovered, stirring occasionally, about 30 minutes or until almost all liquid is absorbed and rice is tender. Add kumara, zucchini, cheese, cream and basil; stir until risotto is hot. *[Best made just before serving.]*

SERVES 4

EGGPLANT FILLED WITH SILVERBEET AND LENTILS

4 medium (1.2kg) eggplants
1 1/2 cups (300g) brown lentils
2 tablespoons olive oil
1 large (200g) brown onion,
   chopped coarsely
1 clove garlic, crushed
400g can tomatoes
1 tablespoon tomato paste
500g silverbeet, trimmed
1/4 cup coarsely chopped fresh
   coriander leaves
1 1/4 cups (125g) coarsely grated
   mozzarella cheese

Halve eggplants lengthways; place in oiled baking dish. Bake, uncovered, in very hot oven about 15 minutes or until just tender. Scoop out flesh from eggplant, leaving a 5mm shell; chop flesh coarsely.

Add lentils to medium pan of boiling water; boil, uncovered, about 15 minutes or until tender, drain.

Heat oil in large pan; cook onion and garlic, stirring, until onion is soft. Add eggplant flesh, lentils, undrained crushed tomatoes, paste and coarsely chopped

silverbeet; cook, stirring, until silverbeet is just wilted. Stir in coriander.

Divide lentil mixture among eggplant shells; sprinkle with cheese. *[Can be made ahead to this stage. Cover; refrigerate overnight.]* Bake, uncovered, in moderate oven about 30 minutes or until browned.

SERVES 4

Left Baked penne with peas, mushrooms and leek
Above Kumara and zucchini risotto
Right Eggplant filled with silverbeet and lentils

BACON MUSHROOM CUSTARDS WITH GARLIC TOAST

Ciabatta is an Italian wood-fired crusty loaf of bread, but you can use any long Italian or French loaf in this recipe.

1 tablespoon olive oil
1 medium (150g) brown onion, chopped finely
2 cloves garlic, crushed
4 bacon rashers, chopped finely
200g button mushrooms, sliced thinly
1 cup (125g) coarsely grated cheddar cheese
8 eggs, beaten lightly
1 tablespoon finely chopped fresh parsley
1/3 cup (80ml) cream

GARLIC TOASTS
30cm loaf ciabatta
1/4 cup (60ml) olive oil
1 clove garlic, crushed

Heat oil in large pan; cook onion and garlic, stirring, until onion is soft. Add bacon and mushrooms; cook, stirring, until mushrooms are tender. Divide mushroom mixture among four oiled 1 1/4-cup (310ml-capacity) ovenproof dishes; top with cheese. Whisk eggs, parsley and cream in large jug; pour over mushroom mixture. Bake custards in moderate oven, uncovered, for about 30 minutes or until set. Serve custards with Garlic Toasts.

Garlic Toasts Cut ciabatta into 2cm slices; brush with combined oil and garlic. Grill until browned both sides.

SERVES 4

MUSHROOM AND BROCCOLI BAKED SPUDS

4 large (1.2kg) potatoes
2 bacon rashers, chopped finely
100g button mushrooms, sliced thinly
1 cup (85g) finely chopped broccoli florets
20g butter
2 tablespoons plain flour
1 cup (250ml) milk
1/2 cup (60g) coarsely grated cheddar cheese

Scrub potatoes, pierce skin; bake potatoes in moderate oven about 1 hour or until tender. When cool enough to handle, cut 1cm off the length of 1 long side of each potato; scoop out the potato flesh, leaving a 5mm shell, place on oven tray.

Cook bacon in medium heated pan, stirring, until browned. Add mushrooms and broccoli; cook, stirring, until broccoli is just tender.

Heat butter in small pan. Add flour; cook, stirring, until mixture thickens and bubbles. Gradually stir in milk; stir until sauce boils and thickens. Remove from heat; stir in half the cheese.

Combine potato flesh, bacon mixture and sauce in large bowl; mix well. Divide the potato mixture among potato shells. *[Can be made ahead to this stage. Cover; refrigerate overnight.]* Sprinkle potatoes with remaining cheese, replace potato tops; bake, uncovered, in moderate oven about 10 minutes or until hot.

Variation Combine potato flesh with a finely chopped green onion, 2 tablespoons each sour cream and sweet chilli sauce. Divide filling among potato shells and serve topped with extra green onion, sour cream and sweet chilli sauce.

SERVES 4

VEGETARIAN CALZONE

2 teaspoons (7g) dried yeast
1 teaspoon sugar
1¹/₂ cups (375ml) warm water
4 cups (600g) plain flour
1 teaspoon salt
¹/₂ teaspoon cracked black pepper
2 tablespoons olive oil
1 cup (125g) coarsely grated cheddar cheese

VEGETABLE FILLING

1 small (230g) eggplant, chopped coarsely
1 tablespoon olive oil
1 large (200g) brown onion, chopped coarsely
2 cloves garlic, crushed
1 medium (200g) red capsicum, chopped coarsely
2 medium (240g) zucchini, chopped coarsely
2 trimmed (150g) celery sticks, chopped coarsely
2 tablespoons tomato paste
¹/₂ cup (125ml) vegetable stock

Whisk yeast, sugar and the water together in small bowl, cover; stand in warm place for about 10 minutes or until the mixture is frothy.

Place flour, salt and pepper in large bowl, stir in yeast mixture and oil; mix to a firm dough. Turn dough onto floured surface; knead about 10 minutes or until smooth and elastic. Place dough in large oiled bowl, cover; stand in warm place about 45 minutes or until doubled in size.

Transfer dough to floured surface; knead until smooth. Divide the dough into 4 pieces; roll each piece to a 24cm round. Spread one side of each round with a quarter of the filling; top with a quarter of the cheese. Fold each round in half to enclose filling; press edges together. Place calzone on oiled oven trays; brush with a little extra oil. Cut 2 small slits on top of each calzone; bake, uncovered, in hot oven about 20 minutes or until browned.

Vegetable Filling Place eggplant in strainer, sprinkle with salt; stand 30 minutes. Rinse eggplant under cold water; drain on absorbent paper. Heat oil in large pan; cook onion and garlic, stirring, until onion is soft. Add eggplant, capsicum, zucchini and celery; cook, stirring, about 5 minutes or until vegetables are soft. Add paste and stock; cook, stirring, until mixture thickens, cool. *[Can be prepared ahead to this stage. Cover; refrigerate overnight or freeze.]*

SERVES 4

Top left Bacon mushroom custards with garlic toast
Left Mushroom and broccoli baked spuds
Above Vegetarian calzone

SPAGHETTI WITH ROASTED VEGETABLES

3/4 cup (180ml) olive oil
3 cloves garlic, crushed
2 medium (400g) red capsicums, sliced thickly
2 medium (400g) yellow capsicums, sliced thickly
1 medium (400g) kumara, chopped coarsely
250g button mushrooms
200g black olives, seeded
500g spaghetti
1/2 cup finely chopped fresh coriander leaves
1 tablespoon finely grated lemon rind
1/4 cup (60ml) lemon juice
100g parmesan cheese, flaked

Heat oil in large pan. Cool 2 minutes, add garlic; cool. Strain mixture over small jug; discard garlic.

Meanwhile, quarter capsicums, remove and discard seeds and membranes. Roast under grill or in very hot oven, skin-side up, until skin blisters and blackens. Cover capsicum pieces in plastic or paper for 5 minutes, peel away skin; slice thinly. *[Can be made ahead to this stage. Cover; refrigerate overnight.]*

Combine kumara and 1 tablespoon of the cooled oil in medium baking dish; bake, uncovered, in moderately hot oven for 15 minutes. Add mushrooms, olives and another tablespoon of the oil; mix well. Bake about 15 minutes or until the mushrooms are tender.

Cook spaghetti in large pan of boiling water, uncovered, until just tender; drain. Just before serving, gently toss pasta in large bowl with capsicum, kumara mixture, remaining oil, coriander, rind and juice; sprinkle with cheese.

SERVES 4

ITALIAN BAKED BEANS

1 cup (200g) dried cannellini beans
1 cup (200g) dried red kidney beans
6 bacon rashers, chopped coarsely
2 large (400g) brown onions, sliced thickly
2 cloves garlic, crushed
1/2 cup (125ml) dry red wine
2 x 400g cans tomatoes
1 cup (250ml) water
1 tablespoon finely chopped fresh basil leaves
1 tablespoon finely chopped fresh parsley
2 cups (140g) stale breadcrumbs
1/4 cup (20g) finely grated parmesan cheese

Place beans in large bowl, cover with water, soak overnight; drain. Rinse beans then add to large pan of boiling water; simmer, uncovered, about 1 hour or until beans are just tender. Drain.

Cook bacon, onion and garlic in large heated pan, stirring, until bacon is browned; drain away excess fat. Add wine; cook, stirring, until wine is reduced by half. Add undrained crushed tomatoes, the water and beans, bring to boil; stir in basil and parsley. *[Can be made ahead to this stage. Cover; refrigerate overnight or freeze.]* Transfer bean mixture to oiled 2-litre (8-cup capacity) ovenproof dish. Sprinkle 1 1/2 cups of the breadcrumbs over the top; bake, uncovered, in moderate oven 40 minutes.

Remove dish from oven; gently stir half of the breadcrumbs into bean mixture. Top with combined remaining breadcrumbs and cheese; bake further 20 minutes or until browned.

SERVES 4 TO 6

Left Spaghetti with roasted vegetables
Below Italian baked beans

CORIANDER GNOCCHI WITH ROAST TOMATO SAUCE

4 large (1.2kg) potatoes, chopped coarsely
1 egg
1 egg yolk
1½ cups finely chopped fresh coriander leaves
1 teaspoon salt
1 teaspoon pepper
1 clove garlic, crushed
1½ cups (225g) plain flour
1¼ cups (100g) finely grated parmesan cheese

ROAST TOMATO SAUCE
700g cherry tomatoes
2 teaspoons coarsely ground black pepper
2 tablespoons vegetable oil
1 medium (150g) brown onion, chopped finely
½ cup (125ml) dry white wine
300ml thickened cream

Boil, steam or microwave potato until tender; drain. Place potato in large bowl; mash until smooth. Stir in egg, egg yolk, coriander, salt, pepper and garlic; using hand, mix in flour. Turn potato mixture onto floured surface; knead lightly about 2 minutes or until smooth. Roll tablespoons of potato mixture into gnocchi-shaped ovals.

Add gnocchi to large pan of boiling water; cook, uncovered, about 3 minutes or until gnocchi float to surface. Remove gnocchi from pan with slotted spoon, place in bowl of iced water until cool; drain. Place gnocchi, in a single layer, on tray; cover, refrigerate. [Can be made ahead to this stage. Cover; refrigerate up to 2 days or freeze.]

Place gnocchi in oiled shallow 2.5-litre (10-cup capacity) ovenproof dish. Pour Roast Tomato Sauce over top; sprinkle with cheese. Bake, uncovered, in moderate oven about 25 minutes or until cheese is browned lightly and gnocchi are hot.

Roast Tomato Sauce Combine tomato, pepper and half the oil in medium baking dish. Bake, uncovered, in moderately hot oven about 10 minutes or until tender.

Meanwhile, heat remaining oil in small pan; cook onion, stirring, until soft. Add wine; cook, stirring, until wine is reduced by half. Stir in cream and tomato; simmer, stirring, until sauce thickens slightly.

SERVES 4

BUTTER BEAN AND VEGETABLE SALAD

4 medium (760g) tomatoes, chopped coarsely
1 large (300g) red onion, sliced thinly
6 green onions, sliced thinly
3 x 300g cans butter beans, rinsed, drained
1 large (350g) red capsicum, chopped coarsely
2 (260g) Lebanese cucumbers, seeded, sliced thickly
200g fetta cheese, crumbled
⅓ cup (80ml) lemon juice
2 tablespoons olive oil
1 clove garlic, crushed
1 teaspoon sugar
½ teaspoon sweet paprika

Combine the tomato, onions, beans, capsicum, cucumber and fetta in a large bowl; gently toss with combined remaining ingredients, just before serving.

SERVES 4

Left Coriander gnocchi with roast tomato sauce
Right from top Butter bean and vegetable salad; Mushroom and rice-filled capsicums

MUSHROOM AND RICE-FILLED CAPSICUMS

You will need ²/₃ cup uncooked calrose rice for this recipe.

2 teaspoons olive oil
1 medium (350g) leek, chopped coarsely
2 cloves garlic, crushed
250g button mushrooms, sliced thickly
1 cup (250ml) chicken stock
2 cups cooked calrose rice
¹/₄ cup (20g) finely grated parmesan cheese
¹/₄ cup (30g) coarsely grated cheddar cheese

2 large (700g) red capsicums
2 large (700g) green capsicums
2 large (600g) red onions
2 large (400g) brown onions
6 green onions
1 tablespoon brown sugar
1 tablespoon malt vinegar

Heat oil in medium pan; cook leek, garlic and mushrooms, stirring, until leek is soft. Add stock; simmer, uncovered, 5 minutes. Combine mushroom mixture in large bowl with rice and cheeses.

Cut off and reserve tops of capsicums; remove and discard seeds and membranes. Divide rice mixture among capsicums; place in large oiled baking dish, replace tops. *[Can be made ahead to this stage. Cover; refrigerate overnight.]*

Cut red and brown onions into wedges; cut green onions into 10cm lengths. Combine red and brown onion in bowl with sugar and vinegar; mix well then place onion around capsicums in baking dish. Bake, uncovered, in moderate oven about 45 minutes or until capsicums are tender and browned lightly. Remove capsicums from baking dish; cover to keep warm. Add green onion to baking dish; bake, uncovered, in hot oven, stirring occasionally, about 10 minutes or until onions are well roasted; serve onions with capsicums.

SERVES 4

BAKED SPINACH, CHEESE AND EGGPLANT

3 medium (1kg) eggplants
vegetable oil, for shallow-frying
1 large (200g) brown onion,
    chopped finely
1 clove garlic, crushed
3 medium (600g) tomatoes,
    chopped coarsely
400g can tomatoes
1 bay leaf
1/2 cup finely chopped
    fresh oregano leaves
2 teaspoons sugar
500g spinach, trimmed
250g ricotta cheese
1 egg, beaten lightly
1/2 teaspoon ground nutmeg
1 clove garlic, crushed, extra
1/2 cup (60g) coarsely grated
    cheddar cheese

CHEESE SAUCE
50g butter
2 tablespoons plain flour
1 1/2 cups (375ml) milk
1 cup (125g) coarsely grated
    cheddar cheese

Cut eggplant into 1cm slices; place on wire rack, sprinkle with salt. Stand 10 minutes. Rinse slices under cold water; drain on absorbent paper.

Heat oil in large pan; shallow-fry eggplant slices, in batches, until browned lightly both sides. Drain eggplant on absorbent paper.

Drain away excess oil from pan; cook onion and half of the garlic, stirring, until onion is soft. Add fresh tomato; cook, stirring, until tomatoes are soft. Add the undrained crushed tomatoes, bay leaf, oregano and sugar; simmer, uncovered, about 15 minutes or until mixture is reduced by half.

Meanwhile, boil, steam or microwave spinach until just wilted; drain. Squeeze excess liquid from spinach; then chop coarsely. Combine spinach, ricotta, egg, nutmeg and remaining garlic in large bowl; mix well.

Spread one-third of the eggplant over base of oiled 3.5-litre (14-cup capacity) ovenproof dish; top with tomato mixture, another one-third of the eggplant then spinach mixture. Top with the remaining eggplant and Cheese Sauce; sprinkle with cheese. *[Can be made ahead to this stage. Cover; refrigerate overnight.]* Bake mixture, uncovered, in moderate oven about 45 minutes or until browned lightly.

Cheese Sauce Melt butter in small pan. Add flour; cook, stirring, until mixture thickens and bubbles. Gradually stir in milk; stir until sauce boils and thickens. Remove from heat; stir in cheese.

SERVES 4

ANGEL-HAIR PASTA WITH CORIANDER AND CHILLI

We used fresh angel-hair pasta here, but any fine pasta, such as vermicelli or spaghettini, can be substituted.

500g fresh angel-hair pasta
1/2 cup (125ml) olive oil
2 bird's-eye chillies, seeded,
    chopped finely
4 cloves garlic, crushed
1 cup finely chopped fresh
    coriander leaves
2 teaspoons salt
2 tablespoons lemon juice
3/4 cup (60g) parmesan
    cheese flakes

Cook pasta in large pan of boiling water, uncovered, until just tender; drain.

Meanwhile, heat oil in large pan; cook chilli and garlic, stirring, about 3 minutes or until fragrant. Remove pan from heat; stir in coriander and salt.

Gently toss coriander mixture with pasta and lemon juice in pan. Just before serving, sprinkle with cheese.

SERVES 4

Left Baked spinach, cheese and eggplant
Right Angel-hair pasta with coriander and chilli

RISOTTO CAKES WITH CRISP BACON AND BASIL CREAM

1 tablespoon olive oil
1 medium (150g) brown onion, chopped finely
1 clove garlic, crushed
3 cups (600g) calrose rice
1 cup (250ml) dry white wine
3 cups (750ml) chicken stock
2 cups (500ml) water
1 cup (125g) frozen peas, thawed
1/3 cup (50g) plain flour
vegetable oil, for shallow-frying
8 bacon rashers

BASIL CREAM

1 tablespoon olive oil
1 small (80g) brown onion, chopped finely
1 clove garlic, crushed
1/2 cup (125ml) dry white wine
600ml cream
1/3 cup coarsely chopped fresh basil leaves

Heat olive oil in large pan; cook onion and garlic, stirring, until onion is soft. Add rice; stir to coat in onion mixture. Stir in wine; cook, stirring, until wine is absorbed. Stir in stock and the water; cook, uncovered, stirring occasionally, until rice is just tender and liquid absorbed. Gently stir in peas; cool 30 minutes.

Shape half-cups of rice mixture into patties; place on tray. *[Can be made ahead to this stage. Cover; refrigerate overnight.]* Coat patties in flour, shake off excess. Heat vegetable oil in large pan; shallow-fry patties, in batches, until browned both sides and heated through. Drain Risotto Cakes on absorbent paper. Drain oil from pan; cook bacon until browned and crisp. Drain on absorbent paper. Serve Risotto Cakes with bacon and Basil Cream.

Basil Cream Heat oil in small pan; cook onion and garlic, stirring, until onion is soft. Add wine; cook, stirring, about 3 minutes or until wine is evaporated. Stir in the cream, bring to boil; simmer, uncovered, about 10 minutes or until sauce thickens slightly. Stir in basil; simmer, uncovered, 5 minutes. Strain sauce over small bowl; discard onion mixture. Return sauce to same pan; simmer, stirring, until hot.

SERVES 4

Right Lentil and vegetable curry
Below Risotto cakes with crisp bacon and basil cream

LENTIL AND VEGETABLE CURRY

1 1/2 cups (300g) red lentils
1 tablespoon vegetable oil
1 large (200g) brown onion, chopped coarsely
2 cloves garlic, crushed
3 teaspoons black mustard seeds
2 teaspoons cumin seeds
2 teaspoons ground turmeric
400g can tomatoes
3 cups (750ml) vegetable stock
1 medium (120g) carrot, chopped coarsely
1 medium (200g) potato, chopped coarsely
1/2 cup (125ml) coconut milk
1/2 cup (60g) frozen peas, thawed

Rinse lentils; drain. Heat oil in large pan; cook onion and garlic, stirring, until onion is soft. Add seeds and turmeric; cook, stirring, until seeds start to pop. Add undrained crushed tomatoes, stock, carrot, potato and lentils; simmer, covered, for about 20 minutes or until vegetables and lentils are just tender. [Can be made ahead to this stage. Cover; refrigerate overnight or freeze.]

Just before serving, add milk and peas; stir over low heat until just hot. Serve with pappadums, if desired.

SERVES 4

Look what's for dessert!

Wickedly rich but decidedly easy on the wallet, these luscious treats make the end of a meal something to look forward to! You'll impress both friends and family with our inspired happy endings

LEMON CURD TART

1¼ cups (185g) plain flour
⅓ cup (55g) icing sugar mixture
¼ cup (30g) almond meal
125g cold butter, chopped
1 egg yolk
1 tablespoon finely grated lemon rind
½ cup (125ml) lemon juice
5 eggs
¾ cup (165g) caster sugar
1 cup (250ml) thickened cream

Blend or process flour, icing sugar, almond meal and butter until crumbly; add egg yolk, process until ingredients just come together. Knead dough on floured surface until smooth, wrap in plastic wrap; refrigerate for 30 minutes. Roll pastry between sheets of baking paper until large enough to line a 24cm round loose-base flan tin. Lift pastry into tin; press into side, trim edge. Cover; refrigerate 1 hour.

Cover pastry with baking paper, fill with dried beans or rice, place on oven tray; bake in moderately hot oven for 15 minutes. Remove paper and beans, bake about 10 minutes or until browned lightly; cool.

Whisk remaining ingredients in large bowl; strain filling into pastry case. Bake in moderate oven about 30 minutes or until filling sets slightly; cool. Refrigerate until cold. *[Best made a day ahead.]* Dust tart with sifted icing sugar just before serving, if desired.

SERVES 8

TOFFEE-TOPPED PROFITEROLES

¾ cup (180ml) water
60g butter
¾ cup (110g) plain flour
3 eggs, beaten lightly
1 cup (220g) sugar
½ cup (125ml) water, extra
⅓ cup (55g) almond kernels
300ml thickened cream

Combine water and butter in small pan; stir over heat until butter melts. Bring to boil; add flour, stir until mixture leaves side of pan and forms a ball.

Transfer mixture to small bowl of electric mixer; add egg, in batches, beating on low speed until smooth between each addition.

Drop heaped teaspoons of mixture about 4cm apart on greased oven trays. Bake in hot oven 10 minutes; reduce heat to moderate, bake profiteroles about 15 minutes or until browned lightly. Slit each profiterole, allowing steam to escape; return to moderate oven about 10 minutes or until profiteroles are crisp. Cool on wire rack. *[Can be kept, in airtight container, up to 5 days or frozen.]*

Meanwhile, combine sugar and extra water in small pan; stir over heat without boiling, until sugar dissolves. Bring to boil; simmer uncovered, without stirring, until toffee is golden.

Cut profiteroles in half; drizzle tops with about half the toffee.

Spread nuts on greased oven tray; pour remaining toffee over nuts. When mixture is set, process until crushed coarsely; stir into whipped cream. Spoon cream mixture into base of each profiterole; gently replace toffeed tops.

SERVES 4

From top Toffee-topped profiteroles; Lemon curd tart

FRUIT-FILLED CHARLOTTES

825g can dark plums in syrup
825g can pear halves in light syrup
1/2 teaspoon mixed spice
1 tablespoon brown sugar
18 slices white bread
100g butter, softened
1 tablespoon caster sugar
1 tablespoon lemon juice

Grease four 1-cup (250ml-capacity) oven-proof dishes.

Drain the plums and pear halves, separately, over a small bowl; reserve syrup. Halve plums; discard seeds. Slice plums and pear halves thinly; combine in medium bowl with mixed spice and brown sugar.

Remove the crusts from bread slices; spread one side of each slice with butter. Cut two 5.5cm rounds from each of two bread slices; place one round, buttered-side down, into each of the prepared dishes. Cut remaining bread slices into 3 strips each. Line side of each dish with bread strips, buttered-side out, slightly overlapping; extend bread 1.5cm above top of dish. Divide fruit mixture among dishes; fold bread over to cover filling, press down firmly to seal.

Place the dishes on oven tray; bake, uncovered, in moderately hot oven about 30 minutes or until just browned lightly.

Meanwhile, combine reserved syrup with caster sugar and juice in medium pan; bring to boil. Simmer, uncovered, about 15 minutes or until syrup thickens slightly. Stand charlottes for 10 minutes before turning onto serving plates; serve with hot syrup.

SERVES 4

STICKY APPLE AND TREACLE CAKE

185g butter
3/4 cup (150g) firmly packed brown sugar
2 eggs
1/4 cup (60ml) treacle
1 teaspoon ground ginger
2 cups (300g) self-raising flour
1/2 cup (125ml) milk
1 large (200g) apple, peeled, chopped

CARAMEL SAUCE
1 cup (200g) firmly packed brown sugar
150g butter, chopped coarsely
1 cup (250ml) cream

Grease deep 20cm round cake pan, line base with baking paper.

Beat butter and sugar in medium bowl with electric mixer until light and fluffy. Add eggs, one at a time, beating well after each addition; stir in the treacle, ginger, flour and milk, in 2 batches, then fold in apple. Spread mixture in prepared pan; bake in moderate oven about 1 hour. Stand cake in pan 5 minutes; turn onto serving plate. Serve cake warm, with Caramel Sauce.

Caramel Sauce Combine ingredients in medium pan; stir over low heat until sugar dissolves and butter melts. Simmer, uncovered, about 5 minutes or until mixture thickens slightly.

SERVES 8

MILE-HIGH ORCHARD PIE

You will need about 3 passionfruit for this recipe.

3 cups (450g) plain flour
1/3 cup (75g) caster sugar
250g butter, chopped
1 teaspoon ground cinnamon
2 eggs
800g can pie apples
825g can pear halves in natural fruit juice
1/4 cup (60ml) passionfruit pulp
1 tablespoon brown sugar

Grease 22cm springform tin.

Process flour, caster sugar, butter and half the cinnamon until just crumbly. Add eggs; process until ingredients just cling together. Knead dough on floured surface until smooth; wrap in plastic wrap, refrigerate 30 minutes.

Press three-quarters of the pastry over base and up side of tin. Wrap remaining pastry in plastic wrap; freeze.

Cover pastry in tin with baking paper, fill with dried beans or rice, place on

oven tray. Bake in moderately hot oven 15 minutes. Remove paper and beans; bake about 10 minutes or until pastry is browned lightly, cool. *[Can be made a day ahead. Keep stored in airtight container.]*

Drain the apple and pear halves separately; pat dry on absorbent paper. Slice pear halves thinly; combine in large bowl with apple, passionfruit pulp and brown sugar. Spoon filling into pastry case. Coarsely grate remaining pastry evenly over filling; sprinkle with remaining cinnamon. Bake in moderate oven about 40 minutes or until browned lightly. Cool pie 15 minutes before removing from tin.

SERVES 8

Plate from Villeroy & Boch

Left Fruit-filled charlottes
Above Sticky apple and treacle cake
Right Mile-high orchard pie

GINGERY PINEAPPLE CAKE WITH CINNAMON CUSTARD

440g can pineapple rings in natural juice
185g butter
^{2}/3 cup (150g) caster sugar
3 eggs
^{1}/3 cup (75g) crystallised ginger, chopped finely
1 cup (150g) plain flour
1 cup (150g) self-raising flour
2 teaspoons ground ginger

CINNAMON CUSTARD
1 cup (250ml) milk
2 egg yolks
^{1}/4 cup (55g) caster sugar
1 teaspoon ground cinnamon

Grease deep 20cm round cake pan, line base and side with baking paper.

Drain pineapple over small bowl; reserve juice. Chop pineapple finely. Beat butter and sugar in medium bowl with electric mixer until light and fluffy. Add eggs, one at a time, beating until just combined after each addition.

Stir in pineapple, reserved juice and crystallised ginger (mixture may curdle). Stir in sifted flours and ground ginger. Spread mixture into prepared pan; bake in moderately slow oven about 1^1/4 hours. Stand cake in pan 5 minutes; turn onto wire rack to cool. Serve with Cinnamon Custard, dusted with icing sugar, if desired.

Cinnamon Custard Bring milk to boil in medium pan. Whisk egg yolks, sugar and cinnamon in medium bowl until thick and pale; gradually whisk into hot milk. Stir over heat, without boiling, until custard mixture thickens slightly.

SERVES 8

CAKE AND BUTTER PUDDING

450g Madeira or butter cake
60g butter
^{1}/2 cup (80g) sultanas
6 egg yolks
1 teaspoon finely grated lemon rind
^{2}/3 cup (150g) sugar
1^1/4 cups (310ml) milk
300ml cream

Grease deep 1.5-litre (6-cup capacity) ovenproof dish.

Cut cake into 2cm slices; spread slices with butter on one side. Place cake slices, overlapping, buttered-side up, in prepared dish; sprinkle over sultanas.

Whisk egg yolks, rind and sugar in medium bowl. Combine milk and cream in medium pan; stir over heat until mixture boils. Gradually whisk hot milk mixture into egg mixture; strain into large jug. Pour custard mixture over cake slices in prepared dish; place in large baking dish, add enough boiling water to come halfway up side of pudding dish. Bake, uncovered, in moderate oven about 40 minutes or until set. *[Best made on day of serving.]* Serve pudding warm or cold, dusted with icing sugar, if desired.

SERVES 6 TO 8

Above Gingery pineapple cake with cinnamon custard
Right Cake and butter pudding

STEAMED CHOCOLATE AND GOLDEN SYRUP PUDDING

185g butter
1/2 cup (100g) firmly packed
  brown sugar
1/2 cup (125ml) golden syrup
1/4 cup (60ml) honey
1/4 cup (60ml) water
2 eggs, beaten lightly
1 1/2 cups (225g) plain flour
1 1/2 cups (225g) self-raising flour
2 tablespoons cocoa powder
1 teaspoon bicarbonate of soda

BUTTERSCOTCH SAUCE
50g butter
300ml thickened cream
1 cup (200g) firmly packed
  brown sugar
2 teaspoons vanilla essence

LOUKOUMADES

*These honey fritters are longed for by
anyone who's ever had them hot, with
a thick coffee and some sheep-milk
yogurt, in an Athens cafe.*

1 1/2 teaspoons (5g) dried yeast
1 cup (250ml) warm water
1/2 teaspoon salt
1 teaspoon sugar
1 1/2 cups (225g) plain flour
vegetable oil, for deep-frying
1/4 cup (60ml) cold water
1 cup (250ml) honey
1/2 teaspoon ground cinnamon

Whisk yeast with the warm water, salt and
sugar in small bowl until dissolved. Place
flour in large bowl; gradually add yeast
mixture, stirring, until mixture forms a
thick smooth batter. Cover; stand in warm
place about 45 minutes or until batter has
doubled in size.

Deep-fry rounded teaspoons of batter
in hot oil, in batches, until browned all
over. Drain loukoumades on absorbent
paper; place in large bowl. Combine the
cold water, honey and cinnamon in small
pan; stir over low heat until almost
boiling. Pour hot syrup over loukoumades;
serve warm or cold.

MAKES 25

Spoons from Sea Style Furnishings

Grease 1.75-litre (7-cup capacity) pudding steamer, line base with baking paper.

Combine butter, sugar, syrup, honey and the water in medium pan; stir over heat until butter melts and sugar dissolves. Bring to boil, remove from heat; cool. Stir in eggs then sifted dry ingredients. Spoon pudding mixture into prepared steamer; cover pudding with greased foil, secure with lid or kitchen string. Place steamer in large pan with enough boiling water to come halfway up side of steamer; simmer, covered, about 2 hours or until pudding is firm, adding more boiling water as necessary. Serve pudding with Butterscotch Sauce.

Butterscotch Sauce Combine all ingredients in medium pan, stir over heat until butter melts. Simmer, uncovered, about 5 minutes or until sauce thickens slightly.

SERVES 6 TO 8

White plate from Country Road Homewares

STRAWBERRY MERINGUE CAKE

5 egg whites
1¹/₄ cups (275g) caster sugar
1 teaspoon ground cinnamon
2 tablespoons strawberry jam
250g strawberries
1 cup (250ml) cream

Grease two 20cm round sandwich pans, line bases and sides with baking paper.

Beat egg whites in medium bowl with electric mixer until soft peaks form; gradually add sugar, beating until dissolved after each addition. Fold in cinnamon and half the warmed, sieved jam. Divide mixture between prepared pans. Dot remaining jam on top of cake mixture in one pan; drag skewer through jam to make a marbled pattern. Place each pan in a shallow baking dish; add enough boiling water to come 1cm up side of each cake pan.

Bake the cakes in slow oven about 30 minutes or until tops are firm to touch and browned lightly. Turn oven off; cool meringue cakes in oven with door ajar.

Process half the strawberries until smooth; slice remaining strawberries thickly. Fold pureed strawberries through whipped cream. Turn plain meringue cake onto serving plate; spread with strawberry cream mixture. Sprinkle cream with slices of strawberries; top with remaining meringue cake, marbled-side up. Refrigerate 2 hours before serving.

SERVES 6 TO 8

Far left Loukoumades
Left Steamed chocolate and golden syrup pudding
Above Strawberry meringue cake

BAKED HONEY AND CINNAMON CHEESECAKE

This cheesecake is best if made a day before serving, to allow the flavour to develop.

1¹/₂ cups (225g) plain flour
125g cold butter, chopped
¹/₄ cup (55g) caster sugar
1 egg yolk
2 tablespoons finely grated lemon rind
3 teaspoons iced water, approximately

CHEESECAKE FILLING
1¹/₄ cups (250g) cottage cheese
250g packaged cream cheese
³/₄ cup (180ml) honey
¹/₂ cup (110g) caster sugar
2 teaspoons ground cinnamon
4 eggs

Grease 22cm springform tin.

Place flour in medium bowl; rub in butter. Add sugar, egg yolk, rind and enough water to make ingredients cling together. Knead gently on floured surface until smooth, wrap dough in plastic wrap; refrigerate 30 minutes.

Roll dough between sheets of baking paper until large enough to line prepared tin. Lift pastry into tin, ease into side, trim edge. Cover; refrigerate 30 minutes.

Cover pastry with baking paper, fill with dried beans or rice, place on oven tray. Bake in moderately hot oven 10 minutes. Remove paper and beans; bake about 10 minutes or until pastry is browned lightly, cool.

Pour Cheesecake Filling into pastry case; bake in moderately slow oven about 1¹/₂ hours or until filling is firm, cool. Cover; refrigerate cheesecake overnight. Just before serving, drizzle with extra honey, if desired.

Cheesecake Filling Beat cheeses, honey, sugar and cinnamon in medium bowl with electric mixer until almost smooth. Add eggs, one at a time, beating well after each addition.

SERVES 8

CREAMED RICE WITH FRUIT COMPOTE

1.25 litres (5 cups) milk
¹/₂ cup (110g) sugar
2 teaspoons rum essence
1 tablespoon vanilla essence
2 cups (400g) calrose rice
¹/₂ cup (60g) flaked almonds, toasted

FRUIT COMPOTE
415g can apricot halves
¹/₂ cup (125ml) water
¹/₃ cup (80ml) orange juice
¹/₄ cup (60ml) lemon juice
¹/₂ cup (110g) sugar
²/₃ cup (110g) seeded prunes
¹/₃ cup (50g) dried currants
2 cinnamon sticks
1 teaspoon finely grated lemon rind

Combine milk, sugar and essences in medium pan; bring to boil, stirring. Gradually stir in rice; cover pan tightly, simmer over very low heat, stirring occasionally, about 25 minutes or until most of the liquid is absorbed. *[Best made just before serving.]*

Serve rice, sprinkled with almonds, with Fruit Compote.

Fruit Compote Drain apricot halves over medium pan. Add the water, juices and sugar; stir over heat, without boiling, until sugar dissolves. Simmer, uncovered, without stirring, for about 5 minutes or until syrup thickens slightly. Add prunes, currants, cinnamon sticks and rind to syrup; simmer, uncovered, stirring occasionally, about 10 minutes or until fruit is plump. Remove from heat, then stir in apricot halves.

SERVES 8

Left Baked honey and cinnamon cheesecake
Top right Rhubarb crumble
Right Creamed rice with fruit compote

RHUBARB CRUMBLE

- 12 large trimmed stems (750g) rhubarb
- 1 cup (220g) caster sugar
- 1 tablespoon lemon juice
- 1/4 cup (35g) self-raising flour
- 50g butter
- 5 (50g) plain sweet biscuits, crushed coarsely
- 1/4 cup (50g) firmly packed brown sugar
- 2 tablespoons desiccated coconut

Grease four 3/4-cup (180ml-capacity) ovenproof dishes.

Cut rhubarb to 5cm lengths; combine rhubarb with caster sugar and juice in large pan. Cook, stirring, about 5 minutes or until sugar dissolves and rhubarb is just tender.

Place flour in medium bowl, rub in butter; stir in biscuits, brown sugar and coconut. Divide rhubarb mixture among prepared dishes; sprinkle with crumble mixture. Place dishes on oven tray; bake, uncovered, in moderate oven about 20 minutes or until browned lightly.

MAKES 4

Cakes and cookies to die for

Keeping their hands out of the cookie jar or their fingers from swiping the frosting will be the hardest part of dealing with these recipes and, while they may all look world-class, making them won't cost you the earth

ZUCCHINI AND ORANGE SLAB CAKE

You will need 3 small zucchini for this recipe.

185g butter
2 teaspoons finely grated orange rind
1 cup (220g) caster sugar
2 eggs
1¹/₂ cups coarsely grated zucchini
¹/₄ cup (60ml) orange juice
1¹/₂ cups (225g) self-raising flour

ORANGE FROSTING
125g butter, softened
2 cups (320g) icing sugar mixture
¹/₄ cup (60ml) orange juice

Grease 19cm x 29cm slice pan, line base with baking paper.

Beat butter, rind and sugar in small bowl with electric mixer until light and fluffy. Add eggs, one at a time, beating until just combined between each addition. Transfer mixture to large bowl; stir in zucchini, juice and flour; spread mixture into prepared pan. Bake in moderate oven about 40 minutes. Stand cake 5 minutes; turn onto wire rack to cool. Top cake with Orange Frosting and, if desired, a little thinly sliced orange rind.

Orange Frosting Beat butter in small bowl with electric mixer until light and fluffy. Gradually beat in icing sugar and juice; beat until frosting is smooth.

FAMILY CHOCOLATE CAKE

³/₄ cup (180ml) water
1 cup (220g) caster sugar
90g butter
2 tablespoons cocoa powder
¹/₂ teaspoon bicarbonate of soda
1 cup (150g) self-raising flour
1 egg, beaten lightly

CHOCOLATE FROSTING
50g butter
2 tablespoons water
¹/₄ cup (55g) caster sugar
³/₄ cup (120g) icing sugar mixture
2 tablespoons cocoa powder

Grease deep 20cm round cake pan, line base with baking paper.

Combine the water, sugar, butter, cocoa and soda in small pan; stir over heat, without boiling, until sugar dissolves. Bring to boil; simmer, uncovered, for 5 minutes.

Transfer mixture to large bowl; cool for 10 minutes. Stir in flour and eggs; beat with wooden spoon until mixture is smooth. Pour mixture into prepared pan; bake in moderate oven about 40 minutes. Stand cake 10 minutes; turn onto wire rack to cool. Spread cake with Chocolate Frosting.

Chocolate Frosting Combine butter, the water and caster sugar in small pan; stir over heat, without boiling, until sugar dissolves. Sift icing sugar and cocoa into medium bowl; gradually stir in hot butter mixture. Cover, refrigerate until thick. Beat with wooden spoon until frosting is spreadable.

From top Family chocolate cake;
Zucchini and orange slab cake

CHOC-COVERED MUESLI BARS

100g butter, chopped
2 cups (180g) rolled oats
1/2 cup (75g) unsalted
   roasted peanuts
1/2 cup (45g) desiccated coconut
1 cup (130g) toasted muesli
1/2 cup (20g) Coco Pops
1 cup (220g) sugar
1/2 cup (125ml) honey
1/4 cup (60ml) water
100g dark chocolate Melts

Grease 20cm x 30cm lamington pan; line base and 2 long sides with baking paper, extending paper 2cm above edge of pan.

Melt butter in large pan; cook oats, peanuts, coconut, muesli and Coco Pops, stirring, about 5 minutes or until mixture is browned lightly.

Combine sugar, honey and the water in small pan; stir over low heat until sugar dissolves. Simmer, uncovered, without stirring, 5 minutes. Add honey syrup to butter mixture; mix well, press into pan. Bake in moderate oven about 25 minutes or until browned. Cool in pan; cut into bar shapes. Drizzle or pipe melted chocolate over one end of each bar, if desired.

CHOCOLATE SPONGE LAMINGTON FINGERS

5 eggs
3/4 cup (165g) caster sugar
1 cup (150g) self-raising flour
2 tablespoons cocoa powder
90g butter, melted
1 tablespoon hot water
2 cups (180g) desiccated coconut

CHOCOLATE ICING

3 cups (480g) icing sugar mixture
1/4 cup (25g) cocoa powder
20g butter, melted
1/2 cup (125ml) milk

Grease 23cm square slab cake pan, line base with baking paper.

Beat eggs and sugar in medium bowl with electric mixer for about 5 minutes or until pale and thick. Sift flour and cocoa together 3 times; gently fold into egg mixture, then gently fold in combined butter and water. Pour the mixture into prepared pan; bake in moderate oven for 30 minutes. Turn sponge immediately onto wire rack to cool.

Cut sponge into 3cm x 7cm fingers; dip sponge fingers into Chocolate Icing, roll in coconut. Place on wire rack to set.

Chocolate Icing Combine sugar, cocoa, butter and milk in large heatproof bowl over pan of simmering water; stir until icing reaches pouring consistency.

MAKES ABOUT 20

COCONUT JAM BISCUITS

2 cups (320g) self-raising flour
1 cup (90g) desiccated coconut
1 cup (220g) caster sugar
200g butter, melted
2 tablespoons milk
1/3 cup (80ml) strawberry jam

Combine flour, coconut and sugar in large bowl; stir in butter and milk. Roll level tablespoons of mixture into balls; place about 8cm apart on greased oven trays. Using floured handle of wooden spoon, press a hollow in each ball about 1cm deep and 1.5cm wide; drop 1/4 teaspoon jam into each hollow. Bake in moderate oven about 15 minutes or until browned lightly. Top jam centres with additional 1/4 teaspoon jam; cool biscuits on trays. Dust with icing sugar, if desired.

MAKES ABOUT 30

Left Choc-covered muesli bars
Top Chocolate sponge lamington fingers
Above Coconut jam biscuits

CARROT AND BANANA SLAB CAKE

You will need 1 large overripe banana for this recipe.

185g butter
1 teaspoon finely grated orange rind
1 cup (220g) caster sugar
2 eggs, beaten lightly
1/2 cup mashed banana
1 medium (120g) carrot, grated coarsely
1/4 cup (60ml) milk
1 1/4 cups (180g) self-raising flour
1/4 cup (35g) plain flour
1 teaspoon mixed spice

CREAM CHEESE FROSTING
90g packaged cream cheese, softened
90g butter, softened
1 cup (160g) icing sugar mixture

Grease 19cm x 29cm slice pan; line base and 2 long sides of pan with baking paper, extending paper 2cm above edge of pan.

Beat butter, rind and sugar in small bowl with electric mixer until light and fluffy. Add eggs, one at a time, beating until just combined after each addition. Transfer mixture to large bowl; stir in banana, carrot, milk and sifted flours and spice, in 2 batches. Spread mixture evenly into prepared pan. Bake in moderate oven about 45 minutes. Stand cake 5 minutes; turn onto wire rack to cool. Top cake with Cream Cheese Frosting and sliced banana, if desired.

Cream Cheese Frosting Beat cheese and butter in small bowl with electric mixer until as white as possible; gradually beat in sugar.

ECONOMICAL FRUIT CAKE

You can use whole blanched almonds rather than Brazil nuts, if you prefer.

4 cups (750g) mixed dried fruit
185g butter
1 cup (200g) firmly packed brown sugar
2 teaspoons finely grated orange rind
1/3 cup (80ml) sweet sherry
1/2 teaspoon bicarbonate of soda
3 eggs, beaten lightly
1 cup (70g) stale breadcrumbs
1 1/2 cups (225g) plain flour
1 tablespoon mixed spice
1/2 cup (85g) Brazil nuts

Line base and side of deep 20cm round cake pan with 3 layers of baking paper, extending paper 5cm above edge of pan.

Combine fruit, butter, sugar, rind and sherry in large pan; stir over heat until butter melts and sugar dissolves. Cover, simmer 5 minutes; remove from heat, stir in soda. Transfer fruit mixture to large bowl, cool; stir in egg, breadcrumbs, flour and spice. Spread mixture evenly into prepared pan; decorate top with nuts, if desired. Bake in slow oven about 2 1/2 hours. Cover hot cake tightly with foil; cool in pan.

Left Economical fruit cake
Above Carrot and banana slab cake

CHUNKY CHOC-CHIP DROP CAKES

125g butter
1/4 cup (50g) firmly packed
  brown sugar
1/4 cup (55g) caster sugar
1/4 cup (35g) self-raising flour
1/4 cup (35g) plain flour
1/2 cup (45g) desiccated coconut
3 cups (90g) corn flakes
1/2 cup (70g) crushed nuts
1/2 cup (95g) dark Choc Bits
1 egg, beaten lightly

Combine butter and sugars in small pan; stir over low heat until butter melts, cool. Combine flours, coconut, corn flakes, nuts and Choc Bits in large bowl; gently stir in butter mixture and egg. Drop level tablespoons of mixture about 5cm apart on greased oven trays. Bake in moderate oven about 12 minutes or until browned lightly. Stand cakes 5 minutes; loosen and cool on trays.

MAKES ABOUT 35

COCONUT BROWNIES

80g butter
100g dark chocolate, chopped
1 1/2 cups (300g) firmly packed
  brown sugar
3/4 cup (180ml) water
1/2 cup (75g) plain flour
1/4 cup (25g) cocoa powder
1/2 cup (45g) desiccated coconut
2 eggs, beaten lightly

Grease 23cm square slab cake pan, line base and sides with baking paper.
Combine butter, chocolate, sugar and the water in medium pan; stir over low heat until butter and chocolate melt. Sift flour and cocoa into large bowl, add coconut; whisk in egg and chocolate mixture. Pour mixture into prepared pan; bake in moderately slow oven for about 1 hour or until firm to touch. Cool brownies in pan before cutting into squares; dust with sifted icing sugar, if desired.

BANANA PARKIN

You will need 2 large overripe bananas for this recipe. It can be made up to a week ahead and kept stored in an airtight container.

125g butter
1/3 cup (75g) firmly packed brown sugar
2/3 cup (160ml) golden syrup
1 1/3 cups (200g) plain flour
2 teaspoons bicarbonate soda
1 tablespoon ground ginger
3/4 cup (65g) minute oats
1 egg, beaten lightly
1 cup mashed banana

Grease deep 19cm square cake pan, line base with baking paper.

Combine butter, sugar and syrup in medium pan; stir over low heat until butter melts. Sift flour, soda and ginger into large bowl, add oats; stir in butter mixture, egg and banana. Pour mixture into prepared pan; bake in moderate oven about 45 minutes. Stand parkin in pan 5 minutes; turn onto wire rack to cool. Serve sliced with butter, if desired.

Top left Chunky choc-chip drop cakes
Left Coconut brownies
Above Banana parkin

HONEY ALMOND BREAD

2 egg whites
1/4 cup (55g) caster sugar
1 tablespoon honey
3/4 cup (110g) plain flour
1/2 teaspoon mixed spice
1/2 cup (80g) almond kernels

Grease 8cm x 26cm bar cake pan; line base and 2 long sides of pan with baking paper, extending paper 2cm above edge of pan.

Beat egg whites, sugar and honey in small bowl with electric mixer until sugar dissolves. Fold in sifted flour and spice, then nuts; spread mixture into prepared pan. Bake in moderate oven for about 30 minutes or until browned lightly. Cool in pan, wrap in foil; stand overnight.

Using serrated knife, slice bread very thinly. Place slices on baking paper-lined oven trays; bake, uncovered, in slow oven about 15 minutes or until crisp.

MAKES ABOUT 50

PASSIONFRUIT CURD SPONGE

4 eggs
2/3 cup (150g) caster sugar
1/3 cup (50g) cornflour
1/3 cup (50g) plain flour
1/3 cup (50g) self-raising flour
300ml cream

PASSIONFRUIT CURD
60g butter
2/3 cup (150g) caster sugar
2 eggs, beaten lightly
1/4 cup (60ml) orange juice
2 teaspoons cornflour
1/2 cup passionfruit pulp

Grease two deep 20cm round cake pans.

Beat eggs and sugar in small bowl with electric mixer about 5 minutes or until pale and thick. Sift flours together 3 times. Transfer egg mixture to large bowl; sift flours over egg mixture, then fold in gently. Divide mixture between the prepared pans; bake in moderate oven 20 minutes. Turn sponges immediately onto wire racks to cool.

Place one sponge on serving plate; spread with half the whipped cream then top cream with half the curd. Top with the second sponge; repeat layering with remaining cream and curd. Refrigerate sponge 30 minutes before serving.

Passionfruit Curd Combine ingredients in top half of double saucepan or in heatproof bowl over pan of simmering water; stir until mixture thickens slightly and coats spoon. Cover curd tightly, refrigerate until cold before using. *[Can be made 2 weeks ahead and kept, covered, in refrigerator.]*

Left Honey almond bread
Right Passionfruit curd sponge

Planning to a budget

An economical approach to every aspect of meal preparation – shopping, storing, preparing, cooking – will determine how much money you spend on food. To enable you to eat better for less, read on...

Commonsense food buying

• Plan and shop for meals in advance to avoid wasting perishable foods.

• Take advantage of specials advertised in your local newspaper or shopping centre then plan a variety of meals to freeze for a later date.

• Marinate meats or poultry, make rissoles or bottle jam or chutney rather than buying them already prepared.

• Be wary of foods that come in expensive packaging. You can't eat the paper or the box – but you're certainly paying for them.

• Organise a co-op arrangement with your neighbours or extended family to buy frequently used foods in bulk from local produce markets or wholesalers.

Shop seasonally

Buying and cooking fresh fruit and vegetables when they're in season is far more economical than searching for them at other times of the year. Some items, such as whole pumpkins or lemons, if stored correctly, can be kept for several months. Many seasonal fruits and vegetables can be frozen, preserved in sugar syrup or pickled.

FRESH FRUIT AND VEGETABLE SEASONAL GUIDE

Many common varieties are not mentioned here because they are available all year.

Produce	Availability
Apricot	November to February
Artichoke, globe	June to November
Asparagus	October to June
Blackberry	December to March
Blueberry	August to May
Raspberry	November to January
Strawberry	Most of the year
Fennel	March to October
Lime	March to September
Mandarin	April to October
Mango	October to March
Nectarine	December to March
Navel oranges	May to October
Valencia oranges	September to April
Peach	November to April
Plum	December to May
Spinach	March to November

Getting the best results from cheaper cuts

• Less expensive cuts of meat and poultry can be just as delicious as the premium ones if you know how to prepare them. It is usually just a case of the right flavouring combinations and longer cooking times but the results are definitely worth the effort.

• Slow cookers work extremely well for cheaper cuts of meat. They do not allow food to reach a high temperature but are cooked over a long period – up to about 8 hours.

• Pressure cookers are another energy-efficient appliance that enhances tougher cuts of meat or chicken. Recipes with a high liquid content usually work best for pressure cookers. Never fill the pressure cooker more than two-thirds full. As a rule, cooking times can be reduced to about a third of conventional stove-top cooking. Thicken with cornflour, etc, and add herbs and green vegetables after the meat or chicken is tender. Simply remove the lid and use the pressure cooker like a saucepan. It is important though, to read the manufacturer's instructions. Always follow all safety precautions.

• Moist cooking methods, such as casseroling and oven-cooking with sufficient liquid to simmer the meat or poultry for the required time, will give satisfactorily tender results.

Freezer know-how

Many of the recipes in this book are suitable to freeze. The following hints will help you to successfully freeze both raw and cooked foods.

• When cooking soups, casseroles, stocks, cakes, etc, cook double quantities and freeze half for another time.

• Cooked food such as casseroles are to be cooled in the refrigerator, then frozen. Freeze in suitable meal-size quantities.

• When freezing items individually [such as prepared fruit and vegetables], place a single layer of food on a flat aluminium tray. Freeze, uncovered, until just firm, then transfer to freezer bags, remove the air and seal.

• Meat or poultry purchased on a styrofoam tray should be repacked before freezing; discard styrofoam tray. Meat and poultry should be sealed

tightly to protect them from freezer burn, dehydration and oxidation of fat.

• Cutting meat or poultry into individual portions, strips or cubes before freezing will save time in meal preparation. Make package as flat as possible so it will defrost quickly when needed.

• Fish and other seafood must be frozen when absolutely fresh.

• Whole fish must be cleaned and gutted before freezing. Pat dry fish and seafood before wrapping.

• Keep seasonings to a minimum; adjust to suit your taste at reheating stage.

• Air should be expelled either by pressing out when wrapping or with a pump so that the food does not dry out, discolour or develop rancid smells or flavours.

• Label all packages and containers with contents' name, weight, or number of portions, and date made.

• Make sure there is plenty of space in the freezer. Cold air needs to circulate around food to freeze it quickly.

• Defrost all food in the refrigerator [allow 10 to 24 hours depending on quantity] or with the aid of a microwave oven on defrost cycle.

• Keep the frozen food turnover constant; don't freeze more of the same thing until you've used up the original. Square and rectangular-shaped packages are the most space-efficient.

What can't I freeze?

• Salad vegetables cannot be frozen if they are intended for use raw.

• Seasoned poultry and rolled meats are not suitable.

• Custards and cream fillings tend to curdle on thawing.

• Gelatine or jelly-like dishes separate when thawed.

• Mayonnaise and creamy-style salad dressings tend to separate when thawed.

• Meringues and meringue toppings tend to both split and weep when thawed.

Packaging

• Plastic bags, oven bags and freezer bags are suitable for most types of food.

• Plastic wrap is suitable for separating food layers, but does not provide sufficient protection for wrapping.

• Food can be wrapped in foil and frozen: be certain the food is securely wrapped.

• Recycle plastic containers such as resealable ice-cream, cottage cheese and yogurt containers. These are all suitable for use in freezing liquids and semi-solid foods.

• Many casserole and baking dishes are suitable for freezer-to-oven-to-table use.

• When using rigid containers, leave 2cm to 5cm space for expansion of the food when it freezes.

FROZEN FOOD STORAGE TIMES *(at -18°C/0°F)*

meat and poultry	4 to 6 months
minced meat or poultry	2 months
fish: oily	3 months
white	6 months
prawns, crabs, lobsters	2 months
fruit and vegetables	6 months
cooked pasta, rice	2 months
cream, cheese, milk	2 to 3 months
butter, margarine	6 months
casseroles, soups, pies	3 months
cakes, biscuits, breads, pastry	3 to 4 months
eggs *(whole, yolks or whites without shell)*	6 months

Pantry basics

A well-stocked pantry, refrigerator and freezer guarantee you will always have the necessary ingredients on hand to throw together a healthy interesting meal... a happier notion than having to resort to the expensive take-away options.

The following list was compiled based on recipes in this book. Once jars and bottles are opened, secure the lids tightly and keep them refrigerated.

Leftover canned food must be transferred to non-reactive containers.

PANTRY
anchovies
barbecue sauce
bay leaves
bicarbonate of soda
biscuits [sweet and savoury]
black bean sauce
breadcrumbs
burghul
canned apricots
canned beans [cannellini, kidney, soya]
canned corn [kernels, creamed]
canned chickpeas
canned passionfruit pulp
canned pears
canned pie apples
canned pineapple
canned plums
canned salmon and tuna
canned tomatoes [puree, paste]
cereals [rolled oats, corn flakes, etc]
chocolate [milk and dark varieties, cocoa]
coconut [desiccated, milk, cream]
cornflour
couscous
curry paste and powder
dried beans [cannellini, haricot, chickpeas, kidney, soya]
chilli [dried flakes, Mexican chilli powder, sweet chilli sauce]
dried fruit [apricots, prunes, sultanas, currants]
dried herbs [tarragon, mixed herbs, oregano, basil, etc]

flour [self-raising, plain, wholemeal self-raising]
French onion soup mix
golden syrup [honey, treacle]
gravy mix
jam [apricot, strawberry, marmalade]
lentils [brown, red, split peas]
mayonnaise
mustard [Dijon, seeded, American-style]
noodles and pastas
oil [vegetable, olive, peanut and sesame]
olives, black
oyster sauce
pappadums
plum sauce
polenta
seeds [poppy, sesame]
rice [calrose, long-grain]
rum essence
soy sauce
spices [cinnamon, coriander, cumin, mixed spice, nutmeg, paprika, pepper, turmeric]
stock cubes [powder or packets]
sugar [brown, caster, icing sugar mixture]
sweet chilli sauce
sweet sherry
Tabasco sauce
tandoori paste
tomato sauce
vanilla essence
vinegar [white, malt, balsamic, cider]
wine [dry red, dry white]
Worcestershire sauce
yeast

REFRIGERATOR
butter
cheese [cheddar, mozzarella, parmesan]
cream
eggs
sour cream
yogurt

FREEZER
bacon
bread
nuts [almonds, Brazil nuts, crushed mixed nuts, peanuts]
pastry [ready-rolled puff, fillo]
stale breadcrumbs
raspberries
vegetables

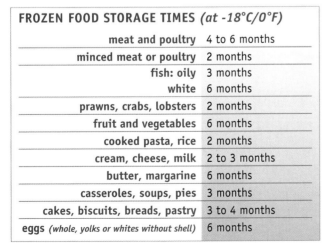

Planning to a budget

Microwave know-how

• Microwave ovens are energy-efficient appliances. They are economical, easy-to-use and time-saving. They heat the food, not your kitchen, and cut down on washing up by minimising the number of dishes used.

• The golden rule for cooking successfully in the microwave oven is to undercook the food slightly, then increase cooking time until the food is cooked as desired. Don't forget to calculate the effects of standing time; most food continues cooking even after the microwave oven stops.

• Variations in cooking times are due to many factors; size, density and water content of the food; size and shape of the cooking vessel; placement of the food in the cooking vessel; and the age, wattage and capacity of the microwave oven.

• For even cooking, fish, chicken, vegetables, etc, should be cut in a similar size and thickness. Foods of uneven thicknesses such as carrots, chicken drumsticks, etc, should be positioned with the thickest part facing the microwave oven walls.

• Microwave ovens as a rule do not cook evenly, so it is important to stir or reposition food during cooking. Generally, if food needs to be turned, covered, stirred, etc, when cooked

Above Ring-shaped moulds ensure cakes cook evenly. To improvise, place a glass in the centre of a round dish.

Above When removing plastic wrap, pull it towards you to prevent the escaping steam from burning you.

Above Foil can be used, in small proportions, as a shield; for instance, to cover chicken wings and drumstick bones to prevent overcooking

Above Shield corners of square or rectangular containers with foil to prevent overcooking.

conventionally, then it is also necessary in the microwave oven.

• Pierce membranes and skins of foods such as potatoes, tomatoes, etc, with a skewer or fork before placing in the microwave oven.

• Do not attempt to deep-fry or shallow-fry in the microwave oven because oil temperatures cannot be controlled.

• Do not attempt to boil eggs in the microwave oven.

Suitable microwave cookware

• A large range of cookware is designed for the microwave oven, but most non-metal dishes are suitable. If in doubt about the suitability of a dish, stand the dish in the oven with a glass of water next to it. Cook on HIGH for 1 minute. If the dish remains cold, it can be used in the microwave oven; if, like the water, the dish gets hot, don't use it in the microwave oven.

• Food cooks more evenly and faster in a shallow, straight-sided round or oval dish rather than in a deeper dish of the same capacity.

• When using plastic wrap to cover food, use caution when you remove the cover as the steam can burn you. The safest way to remove the plastic wrap is to pull it towards you, letting steam escape away from you.

• When reheating food, cover it so that it will retain moisture. Oven bags are good to use in the microwave oven. Secure them loosely with a rubber band, string or a strip cut from the top of the bag itself. Don't use metal ties even if covered in paper, plastic or foil.

GLOSSARY

tat soi

bok choy

choy sum

ASIAN GREEN VEGETABLES
The same vegetables can be called by more than one name, often causing confusion. Here we have listed many of the alternative names.
Bok choy (bak choy, pak choi, Chinese white cabbage, Chinese chard) mild, fresh mustard taste; use stems and leaves.
Choy sum also known as flowering bok choy or flowering white cabbage.
Tat soi (rosette pak choy, tai gu choy, Chinese flat cabbage) a variety of bok choy, developed to grow close to the ground for protection from frost.

BAKING POWDER
a raising agent consisting mainly of 2 parts cream of tartar to 1 part bicarbonate of soda (baking soda).

BEANS
Haricot small, dried white bean similar in appearance and flavour to other Phaseolus vulgaris, great northern, navy and cannelloni beans.
Cannellini (butter) small white beans.
Red kidney beans have a floury texture and fairly sweet flavour; colour can vary from pink to maroon.
Soy small oval bean ranging in colour from yellow to black. Used extensively in vegetarian cooking due to high protein content. Source of many by-products such as soy sauce, tamari, miso, tofu and soy milk.

BEEF
Blade roast whole piece cut from the forequarter (shoulder).
Blade steak from the shoulder blade area.
Bones chuck and brisket bones from the forequarter. Shin bones from the hindquarter. Use for soups or stocks.
Chuck steak from the neck.
Corned Silverside cut from the outside of the upper leg and cured.
Gravy shin beef without the bone.
Mince also known as ground beef.
Oxtail tail from a beef carcass. Requires long slow cooking to achieve a tender result.
Round steak boneless cut from the hindquarter.

BICARBONATE OF SODA
also known as baking soda.

BREADCRUMBS
Stale 1- or 2-day-old bread made into crumbs by blending or processing.

BURGHUL
also known as bulghur wheat; hulled steamed wheat kernels that, once dried, are crushed into various size grains. Used in Middle-Eastern dishes such as kibbeh and tabouleh.

BUTTER
use salted or unsalted ("sweet") butter; 125g is the equivalent of 1 stick butter.

BUTTERMILK
low-fat milk cultured to give a slightly sour, tangy taste; low-fat yogurt can be substituted.

CAJUN SEASONING
a commercially prepared spice mixture containing salt, paprika, cayenne, garlic, onion, basil, white pepper, wheat starch, fennel, pepper and thyme.

CAPSICUM
also known as bell pepper or, simply, pepper. Seeds and membranes should be discarded before use.

CHICKPEAS
also called garbanzos, hummus or channa; an irregularly round, sandy-coloured legume used extensively in Mediterranean and Latin cooking.

CHILLIES
available in many different types and sizes. Use rubber gloves when seeding and chopping fresh chillies as they can burn your skin. Removing seeds and membranes lessens the heat level.

CHOCOLATE
Choc Bits also known as chocolate chips and chocolate morsels; available in milk, white and dark chocolate. Made of cocoa liquor, cocoa butter, sugar and an emulsifier, these hold their shape in baking and are ideal for decorating.
Dark eating chocolate; made of cocoa liquor, cocoa butter and sugar.
Melts available in milk, white and dark chocolate. Made of sugar, vegetable fats, milk solids, cocoa powder, butter oil and emulsifiers, these are good for melting and moulding.

COCOA
cocoa powder.

COCONUT
Desiccated unsweetened, concentrated, dried shredded coconut.
Milk pure, unsweetened coconut milk available in cans and cartons.
Milk powder coconut milk that has been dehydrated and ground to a fine powder.

COCO POPS
chocolate-flavoured puffed rice eaten as breakfast cereal.

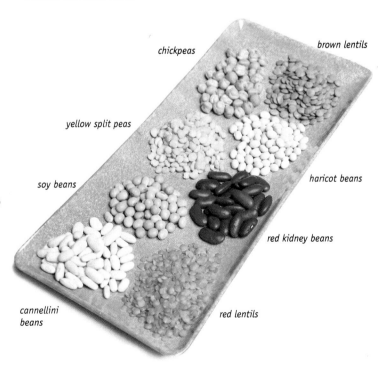

chickpeas *brown lentils*

yellow split peas

soy beans *haricot beans*

red kidney beans

cannellini beans *red lentils*

red onion

green onion

brown onion

CORN FLAKES crisp flakes of corn. A universally popular breakfast cereal.

CORNFLOUR also known as cornstarch; used as a thickening agent in cooking.

COUSCOUS a fine, grain-like cereal product, originally from North Africa, made from semolina.

CREAM
Fresh (minimum fat content 35%) also known as pure cream and pouring cream; has no additives, unlike commercially thickened cream, which uses gelatine.
Sour (minimum fat content 35%) a thick, commercially-cultured soured cream good for dips, toppings and baked cheesecakes.
Thickened (minimum fat content 35%) a whipping cream containing a thickener such as gelatine.

CRUSHED MIXED NUTS a commercially packaged finely chopped unsalted roasted peanuts.

CUSTARD POWDER packaged vanilla pudding mixture.

EGGPLANT also known as aubergine.

ESSENCES also known as extracts; the by-product of distillation of plants.

FLAKE small flaky chocolate bar.

FLOUR
Plain an all-purpose flour, made from wheat.
Plain Wholemeal plain also known as all-purpose wholewheat flour, has no baking powder added.

Self-raising plain flour sifted with baking powder in the proportion of 1 cup flour to 2 level teaspoons baking powder.

FRENCH ONION SOUP MIX a packaged soup mix often added to meat and poultry dishes for flavour and as a thickening agent.

FRESH HERBS we have specified when to use fresh or dried herbs. We used dried (not ground) herbs in the proportion of 1:4 for fresh herbs; use 1 teaspoon dried herbs instead of 4 teaspoons (1 tablespoon) chopped fresh herbs.

GINGER
Crystallised ginger poached in a sugar syrup then rolled in sugar. Used as a flavouring for cakes and biscuits.
Fresh also known as green or root ginger; the gnarled root of a tropical plant. Can be kept, peeled, covered with dry sherry in a jar and refrigerated, or frozen in an airtight container.

GOLDEN SYRUP a by-product of refined sugarcane; pure maple syrup or honey can be substituted.

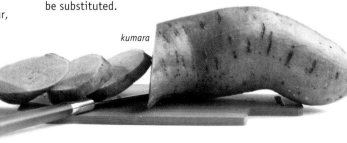

kumara

GRAVY POWDER a flour-based product used to colour and thicken sauces, gravies, etc.

JAM also known as preserves or conserve; most often made from fruit.

KUMARA Polynesian name of orange-fleshed sweet potato often confused with yam.

LAMB
Corned leg a leg of lamb that has been cured in a seasoned brine.
Diced cubed lean meat.
Shank forequarter leg.
Mince ground lamb.

LARD fat obtained from melting down and clarifying pork fat; available packaged.

LENTILS many different varieties of dried legumes, often identified by and named after their colour.

MADEIRA CAKE rich plain cake flavoured with lemon.

MILK we used full-cream homogenised milk unless otherwise specified.

MIXED DRIED FRUIT a combination of sultanas, raisins, currants, mixed peel and cherries.

OATS
Minute rolled oats that have been cut and rolled thinner to reduce cooking time.
Oatmeal whole oat grains that have been cut several times but not gone through rolling process.
Rolled whole oat grains are steamed and flattened to produce rolled oats. Generally used to make porridge or in baking.

OIL
Vegetable any of a number of oils sourced from plants rather than animal fats.

ONION
Brown most common variety, medium to large in size with light brown skin. Strong in flavour, used in soups, casseroles and stock.
Green also known as scallion or (incorrectly) shallot; an immature onion picked before the bulb has formed, having a long, bright-green edible stalk.
Red also known as Spanish, red Spanish or Bermuda onion; a sweet-flavoured, large, purple-red onion that is particularly good eaten raw in salads.

PAPPADUM a crisp wafer-thin Indian bread made from lentil flour; sold in various flavours such as chilli, black pepper, garlic and caraway.

PASSIONFRUIT also known as granadilla; a small tropical fruit, native to Brazil, comprised of a tough outer skin surrounding edible black sweet-sour seeds.

PIPIES a bi-valve mollusc; small creamy grey shell, similar in appearance and texture to baby clam or vongole.

PLAIN SWEET BISCUITS commercially prepared small, thin, flour-based crisp sweet cakes. Un-iced pastry-like biscuits also known as cookies.

POLENTA a flour-like cereal made of ground corn (maize); similar to cornmeal but coarser and darker in colour; also the name of the dish made from it.

PORK
American-style spareribs well-trimmed mid-loin ribs.
Hand pickled cut from the fore end of the pig. Usually sold on the bone and has been cured in a seasoned brine.
Mince also known as ground pork.
Neck sometimes called pork scotch, boneless cut from the foreloin.

PORK & VEAL MINCE a combination of finely ground fresh pork and veal.

PUMPKIN sometimes used interchangeably with the word squash, the pumpkin is

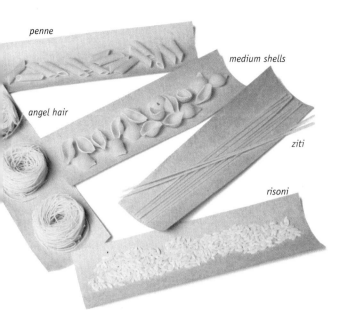

penne

medium shells

angel hair

ziti

risoni

a member of the gourd family used in cooking, both as one of many ingredients in a dish or eaten on its own. Various types can be substituted for one another.

REDCURRANT JELLY a preserve made from redcurrants used as a glaze for desserts and meats or in sauces.

RHUBARB most often used as fruit but botanically a vegetable. Celery-like in appearance, stalks are pinkish red, leaves are green. Rhubarb has an intense, tart flavour.

RICE
Basmati a white, fragrant long-grained rice. It should be washed several times before cooking.
Calrose a medium-grain rice that is extremely versatile; can substitute for short- or long-grain rices if necessary.
Long-grain elongated grain, remains separate when cooked; most popular steaming rice in Asia.

RISONI rice-sized, teardrop-shaped pasta.

SAUCES
Barbecue a spicy, tomato-based sauce used to marinade, baste or as an accompaniment.
Black bean a Chinese sauce made from fermented soy beans, spices, water and wheat flour.

Oyster Asian in origin, this rich, brown sauce is made from oysters and their brine, cooked with salt and soy sauce, and thickened with starches.
Plum a thick, sweet and sour dipping sauce made from plums, vinegar, sugar, chillies and spices.
Soy made from fermented soy beans. Several variations are available in most supermarkets and Asian food stores. **Salt-reduced:** we used a soy sauce with 46% of the salt removed after it is made.
Sweet chilli is a comparatively mild Thai-type sauce made from red chillies, sugar, garlic and vinegar.
Tomato also known as ketchup or catsup; a flavoured condiment made from slow-cooked tomatoes, vinegar and spices.
Worcestershire a thin, dark-brown spicy sauce used as a seasoning for meat, gravies and cocktails and as a condiment.

SUGAR we used coarse, granulated table sugar, also known as crystal sugar, unless otherwise specified.
Brown an extremely soft, fine granulated sugar retaining molasses for its characteristic deep colour and flavour.
Caster also known as superfine or finely granulated table sugar.

Dark brown is white sugar combined with molasses. Is soft and moist in texture and has a more intense molasses flavour and colour than regular brown sugar.
Icing sugar mixture also known as confectioners' sugar or powdered sugar; granulated sugar crushed together with a small amount (about 3%) of cornflour added.
Raw natural brown granulated sugar.

SAUSAGE MINCE ground pork or other meat mixed with fat, salt and various seasonings, and sold without the sausage casing; used for meatloaf and terrines.

SPINACH
English correct name for spinach; the green vegetable often called spinach is correctly known as Swiss chard, **silverbeet** or seakale. Delicate, crinkled green leaves on thin stems; high in iron, it's good eaten raw in salads or steamed gently on its own.

STOCK 1 cup (250ml) stock is the equivalent of 1 cup (250ml) water plus 1 crumbled stock cube (or 1 teaspoon stock powder). If you prefer to make your own fresh stock, see recipes on page 118.

TOFU also known as bean curd, an off-white, custard-like product made from the "milk" of crushed soy beans; comes fresh as soft or firm, and processed as fried or pressed dried sheets. Leftover fresh tofu can be refrigerated in water (which is changed daily) up to 4 days. Silken tofu refers to the method by which it is made – where it is strained through silk.
Bean curd pouches pockets of bean curd (tofu) which can be opened out to take a filling. Available from Asian food stores.

TOMATO PASTE triple-concentrated tomato puree used to flavour soups, stews, sauces and casseroles.

TREACLE thick, dark syrup not unlike molasses; a by-product from sugar refining.

YEAST a 7g (1/4oz) sachet of dried yeast (2 teaspoons) is equal to 15g (1/2oz) compressed yeast if you are substituting one type for the other.

YELLOW SPLIT PEAS also known as field peas, this legume is suitable for purees, dhals and soups.

ZUCCHINI also known as courgette.

silverbeet

spinach

INDEX

MAKE YOUR OWN STOCK

These recipes can be made up to 4 days ahead and stored, covered, in the refrigerator. Be sure to remove any fat from the surface after the cooled stock has been refrigerated overnight. If the stock is to be kept longer, it is best to freeze it in smaller quantities.

Stock is also available in cans or tetra packs. Stock cubes or powder can be used. As a guide, 1 teaspoon of stock powder or 1 small crumbled stock cube mixed with 1 cup (250ml) water will give a fairly strong stock. Be aware of the salt and fat content of stock cubes and powders and prepared stocks.

All stock recipes make about 2.5 litres (10 cups).

BEEF STOCK
2kg meaty beef bones
2 medium (300g) onions
2 sticks celery, chopped
2 medium (250g) carrots, chopped
3 bay leaves
2 teaspoons black peppercorns
5 litres (20 cups) water
3 litres (12 cups) water, extra

Place bones and unpeeled chopped onions in baking dish. Bake in hot oven about 1 hour or until bones and onions are well browned. Transfer bones and onions to large pan, add celery, carrots, bay leaves, peppercorns and water, simmer, uncovered, 3 hours. Add extra water, simmer, uncovered, further 1 hour; strain.

CHICKEN STOCK
2kg chicken bones
2 medium (300g) onions, chopped
2 sticks celery, chopped
2 medium (250g) carrots, chopped
3 bay leaves
2 teaspoons black peppercorns
5 litres (20 cups) water

Combine all ingredients in large pan, simmer, uncovered, 2 hours; strain.

FISH STOCK
1.5kg fish bones
3 litres (12 cups) water
1 medium (150g) onion, chopped
2 sticks celery, chopped
2 bay leaves
1 teaspoon black peppercorns

Combine all ingredients in large pan, simmer, uncovered, 20 minutes; strain.

VEGETABLE STOCK
2 large (360g) carrots, chopped
2 large (360g) parsnips, chopped
4 medium (600g) onions, chopped
12 sticks celery, chopped
4 bay leaves
2 teaspoons black peppercorns
6 litres (24 cups) water

Combine all ingredients in large pan, simmer, uncovered, 1¹/₂ hours; strain.

FACTS AND FIGURES

Wherever you live, you'll be able to use our recipes with the help of these easy-to-follow conversions. While these conversions are approximate only, the difference between an exact and the approximate conversion of various liquid and dry measures is but minimal and will not affect your cooking results.

DRY MEASURES

Metric	Imperial
15g	1/2oz
30g	1oz
60g	2oz
90g	3oz
125g	4oz (1/4lb)
155g	5oz
185g	6oz
220g	7oz
250g	8oz (1/2lb)
280g	9oz
315g	10oz
345g	11oz
375g	12oz (3/4lb)
410g	13oz
440g	14oz
470g	15oz
500g	16oz (1lb)
750g	24oz (11/2lb)
1kg	32oz (2lb)

LIQUID MEASURES

Metric	Imperial
30ml	1 fluid oz
60ml	2 fluid oz
100ml	3 fluid oz
125ml	4 fluid oz
150ml	5 fluid oz (1/4 pint/1 gill)
190ml	6 fluid oz
250ml	8 fluid oz
300ml	10 fluid oz (1/2 pint)
500ml	16 fluid oz
600ml	20 fluid oz (1 pint)
1000ml (1 litre)	13/4 pints

HELPFUL MEASURES

Metric	Imperial
3mm	1/8in
6mm	1/4in
1cm	1/2in
2cm	3/4in
2.5cm	1in
5cm	2in
6cm	21/2in
8cm	3in
10cm	4in
13cm	5in
15cm	6in
18cm	7in
20cm	8in
23cm	9in
25cm	10in
28cm	11in
30cm	12in (1ft)

MEASURING EQUIPMENT

The difference between one country's measuring cups and another's is, at most, within a 2 or 3 teaspoon variance. (For the record, 1 Australian metric measuring cup holds approximately 250ml.) The most accurate way of measuring dry ingredients is to weigh them. When measuring liquids, use a clear glass or plastic jug with the metric markings.

If you would like to purchase The Australian Women's Weekly Test Kitchen's metric measuring cups and spoons (as approved by Standards Australia), turn to page 120 for details and order coupon. You will receive:

- a graduated set of 4 cups for measuring dry ingredients, with sizes marked on the cups.
- a graduated set of 4 spoons for measuring dry and liquid ingredients, with amounts marked on the spoons.
- 1 teaspoon: 5ml
- 1 tablespoon: 20ml.

Note: North America and UK use 15ml tablespoons. All cup and spoon measurements are level.

How To Measure

When using graduated metric measuring cups, shake dry ingredients loosely into the appropriate cup. Do not tap the cup on a bench or tightly pack the ingredients unless directed to do so. Level top of measuring cups and measuring spoons with a knife. When measuring liquids, place a clear glass or plastic jug with metric markings on a flat surface to check accuracy at eye level.

We use large eggs having an average weight of 60g.

OVEN TEMPERATURES

These oven temperatures are only a guide. Always check the manufacturer's manual.

	C° (Celsius)	F° (Fahrenheit)	Gas Mark
Very slow	120	250	1
Slow	150	300	2
Moderately slow	160	325	3
Moderate	180 - 190	350 - 375	4
Moderately hot	200 - 210	400 - 425	5
Hot	220 - 230	450 - 475	6
Very hot	240 - 250	500 - 525	7

Life's easier with these great Home Library gifts

Protect your favourite cookbooks and keep them clean, tidy and within easy reach with this smart vinyl folder*. PLUS you can follow our recipes perfectly with a set of measuring cups and spoons, as used in the Women's Weekly Test Kitchen.

TO ORDER YOUR BOOK HOLDER OR MEASURING SET:

Price: Book Holder $11.95 (Australia); elsewhere $A21.95.
Metric Measuring Set $5.95 (Australia); $8.00 (New Zealand); $A9.95 elsewhere
prices include postage and handling. This offer is available in all countries.

Phone: Have your credit card details ready. Sydney: (02) 9260 0035; **elsewhere in Australia:** 1800 252 515 (free call, Mon-Fri, 8.30am-5.30pm) or FAX your order to (02) 9267 4363 or MAIL your order by photocopying or completing the coupon below.

Payment: **Australian residents:** we accept the credit cards listed, money orders and cheques. **Overseas residents:** we accept the credit cards listed, drafts in $A drawn on an Australian bank, and also English, New Zealand and U.S. cheques in the currency of the country of issue. Credit card charges are at the exchange rate current at the time of payment.

Complete coupon and fax or post to:
AWW Home Library Reader Offer, ACP Direct, PO Box 7036, Sydney NSW 1028.